# Making the Difference

PAT DIXON

# Making the Difference

*Women and Men in the Workplace*

HEINEMANN : LONDON

First published in Great Britain 1993
by William Heinemann Ltd
an imprint of Reed Consumer Books Ltd
Michelin House, 81 Fulham Road, London SW3 6RB
and Auckland, Melbourne, Singapore and Toronto

Copyright © 1993 by Pat Dixon

A CIP catalogue record for this book
is available at the British Library
ISBN 0434 19232 5

Typeset by CentraCet, Cambridge
Printed in Great Britain
by Clays Ltd, St Ives PLC

# Contents

# Acknowledgments

Many thanks . . .

. . . to Chris, Tom and Jack Bertram, not only for keeping the household afloat while I spread papers all over the kitchen table, but for remaining constantly involved, interested and optimistic, no matter what the provocation. This book is for you, with love.

. . . to my mother and father, for setting my feet on the path to here, and my brothers, for trying manfully to help me keep a sense of perspective.

. . . to my friends (especially Christine Haydon-Deschenaux, Becky Carney, and above all Lynda Appleby) for space or a listening ear – whichever I needed, whenever I needed it, and whatever their own agendas at the time.

. . . to Lucy Grey, for her enthusiastic search of the literature on women at work.

. . . to all my colleagues at John Nicholson Associates Ltd – John Nicholson, Cathy Walton, Fiona Thompson, Carmen Harris, Aryanne Oade, Helen Fisher, Mike Ratsey, and especially John McBride – for their warm amalgam of tea, sympathy, time, encouragement, criticism, support, research, proof-reading and illumination.

. . . to Elsbeth Lindner, for her timely expressions of confidence and her direct and constructive feedback.

. . . and, last but emphatically not least, to the many people all over Britain who, formally in interviews or informally over a pint, generously gave up their time to talk about women and men in the workplace. Without their insights there would have been no book.

# Foreword

I'm a working woman. Saying this could be a neat device for turning off two sets of people who are crucial to this book: women who aren't in paid employment and men. One woman with a husband, three children and an elderly mother protested: 'Do me a favour! I work very hard, but I don't get a wage packet for it. Don't talk about "working women" when you mean "wage-earning women".' The point is well taken – but the available terminology is either misleading or clumsy. I shall resort to quotation marks where appropriate. As for the second group: one of the directors of a national distribution company outlined to me men's scepticism about the way women portray some aspects of men at work. 'Advise me, then,' I said: 'How can I get men to suspend disbelief long enough to consider the evidence?' His reply was instantaneous. 'Easy,' he said. 'Don't mention women at all until page 20.' Another senior manager was even blunter. 'Get a man to write the book,' he said.

This forceful opposition to the idea of discussing women at work was the prime motivation for writing this book. I wanted to distinguish myth from reality, uncover the meaning behind the stereotypes, and find out if, and how, women and men can work together more profitably. I've been a 'working woman' for many years, but I'm still not completely sure how to behave at work. It seems to be men's rules that govern the relationships, the routes, the rewards. From years of observation I've learned many of these rules, but funny things can happen when I apply them – and I'm hesitant about flouting or changing them. I end up feeling anxious or angry or frustrated about what's going on. I'm glad I'm a woman, and I relish challenge – but it's unnecessarily hard being a 'working woman' in a man's world.

On a good day I feel like a tourist who's picked up enough of the language to pass as a native, if only temporarily and for specialised moments. On a bad day I feel like an outcast amongst beings whose ways and aims I haven't the ghost of a chance of understanding, let alone working with. Mostly I feel as though I'm trudging solo through a half-mapped jungle – occasionally being ambushed, and reacting like some sort of guerrilla fighter in a brief affray. What I really want is to be a paid-up inhabitant of a world that's designed for me as well, where I have a better than evens chance of understanding and being understood, so that I can concentrate on the job I'm paid to do. (Overkill? Not to anyone who has ever been in any kind of minority or undervalued group. If you haven't, this is where the suspension of disbelief comes in.).

I was born at the beginning of the second half of this century, and I expect I'm about halfway through my 'working life'. If I'd been born fifty years earlier, I couldn't have counted on getting a vote, further education or an interesting job. By the time I entered the workforce in the early Seventies, women had come a long way. But even then, as a marginal suburban hippy who had heard of Germaine Greer, I held firm to traditional expectations. I would be a consort for my husband, whose life pattern would dictate mine. Teaching was the ideal career for me because it was safe: there were plenty of other women doing it, and I could have the holidays off to look after my children.

It didn't work out that way. Twenty years on I find myself with the sort of working history many women of my generation describe. From one point of view you could call it scrappy, involving spells in education and retailing, interspersed with periods of home-making. From another you could say it was evidence of spectacular adaptability and skill. In my time I've been an employee, a boss, a full-time housewife and mother of two sons, a part-timer, an entrepreneur and a consultant. I'm old enough to remember the bad old days at work and be moderately grateful for progress, and young enough to have a personal interest in a brighter future for women (and men) both inside and outside organisations.

Currently I'm a business psychologist in a Human Resources

consultancy. We interview people in different jobs and at all levels right across organisations; write reports on our findings; develop and implement programmes of various kinds. They might include workshops in Personal Development for ten senior managers, or Team-Building for fifteen people who habitually work together, or Customer Service for forty people from a mixture of jobs. We ask questions and set up exercises which prompt people to examine how their organisations function, the good and bad aspects of the jobs they do, and the place of work in their lives. I've been able to listen to men and women from every level of all kinds of different organisations. And I have picked up a sense of enormous waste – actual and impending – because of unconfronted issues, and wires which remain inextricably crossed. The mixture of differences ought to release energies and talents which will lift working performances to new heights of excellence. Instead, all too often those energies are ignored – or turn inwards and are frittered away on sterile debate about the difficulties of difference. Individuals are hamstrung, and organisations deny themselves a substantial resource.

People may think I'm making a song and dance about all this. Perhaps I'm suffering from some fatal flaw of personality, or a ridiculous chip on the shoulder, or an inability to change with the times and combat what my upbringing, my education and my early experience taught me to expect of life and work. But if I am, I'm not alone. It turns out that plenty of 'working women' feel awkward or angry in a man's world; it's not only women of forty-something, but older and younger ones, too, who recount experiences I recognise; and some women describe obstacles and problems which I have never encountered. Men also have troubles, some involving women as they take a higher profile in the workplace and wake up a lot of sleeping dogs.

Hence this book, which is about some of the problems and opportunities which cause grief and hope from time to time when men and women are gathered together at work. I'm approaching it neither primarily as a psychologist (though I quote research where I can find it) nor as a management consultant (though I include first-hand accounts of relevant experiences in the workplace, told by a wide range of people across many organisations). The prompt for the book was a personal one. I'd like to open a window on to the working world, to give the perspective of a woman who finds it often confusing, sometimes damaging, occasionally terrific.

Of course, work takes place in a context which includes a whole raft of 'Big Issues', mostly driven by men: economics, the law and politics. My focus, however, is simply on interactions between men and women: at work, and as they affect work. Much more microscopic than the Government or the Economy – yet, actually, in the long run, of greater import. We are all the products of interactions between men and women. You could say, at the most basic level, that achieving such interactions is what we're here for: the survival of the species.

Having a professional agenda doesn't magically wipe out the eternal dialogue between women and men. All its elements remain: how we talk to one another; how we look; how we react to new situations; what we do when we can't get what we want; how we try to convince people to behave differently; how we manage when we have children to consider; what happens to us under the assault of love or chemistry. The professional agenda adds a further dimension to the dance. Mystery, invitation, misunderstanding, enjoyment, frustration can be compounded by the demands of the task. If we're going to make an effort to fulfil the potential of individuals, and to ensure a level of achievement which produces both personal job satisfaction and the most effective results for organisations, we need to ask: What's going on between men and women at work? Part One of this book examines that question, and Part Two addresses the one which logically follows: What, if anything, should we be doing about it?

## PART ONE

# What's going on between men and women at work?

# 1 Women in the Workplace

## Where are we now?

Thirty years ago men were lords of the working world, and a few women did well in it, if they were lucky, bold and very, very good. Twenty years ago protests and a desire for social justice prompted the Sex Discrimination Act and the Equal Pay Act – mechanisms aimed at providing equal opportunities for all, and giving women the chance to catch up.

How did we do? Here is a small bald sample of statistics concerning men and women in the British workplace at the beginning of the 1990s.

- About half the general population is female, and women comprise about 43% of the 'working' population. However, the spread is far from even, either across occupations or up and down organisational levels.
- About two-thirds of the people in sales, clerical, secretarial and service functions are women. However, only a quarter of managers are women, a third of professionals, a quarter of machine operatives, and a tenth of skilled manual workers.
- On average, in the early Nineties, men worked 43 hours per week, and women just over 30 – the highest difference between the sexes in Europe.
- *New Earnings Survey* figures released by the Department of Employment in September 1991 showed 13 million men and 6.5 million women in full-time employment, and 1.5 million men and 5 million women in part-time work. The average weekly wage for men was £319, and for women £222.

- At the end of 1991, according to *Women in Britain* – a report from the Central Office of Information – certain occupations seemed to remain largely masculine. Law, for instance: one of the 27 Appeal Judges was a woman; 2 out of 83 High Court Judges; 20 of 428 circuit judges. Only 44 MPs out of 650 were women – a puny 7 per cent bettered almost everywhere else in Europe. (In the 1992 General Election the number increased to 60 – still less than 10 per cent). Four per cent of middle and senior management posts were held by women throughout industry. One engineer in a hundred was a woman. Female surveyors, architects and chartered accountants represented less than one-tenth of the total. Three per cent of surgeons were women – and yet in 1991, for the first time, the number of women entering medical school was higher than the number of men.
- *Crawford's Directory of City Connections 1992* gave figures for senior executives on the boards of companies on the quoted and unlisted securities markets. Of a total of 1633 chairpersons six were women – one woman for every 271 men. There was one female Chief Executive or Managing Director for every 200 or so male ones. One Company Secretary in 20 was a woman. Of all the very senior posts mentioned, just over 2 per cent were held by women.
- A report on the National Health Service in early 1992 revealed that 80 per cent of its 1,150,000 employees were women. But only 30 per cent of non-executive members of health authorities, one of the 14 chairmen of regional authorities, and three of the 57 chairmen of trust hospitals, were women.
- The Institute of Directors surveyed 200 of its women members in 1992. Only 58 per cent were mothers. No parallel research was done on equivalent males, but the Chairman of the Institute thought it certain that more than 58 per cent of male Directors had children.

## It's a man's world

What have we got in the early Nineties? Still a man's world, apparently. The conclusions we can draw from the current figures don't materially differ from those of the Seventies.

- There are enough women in the workforce to make them a vital factor in organisational effectiveness.

- Leaders tend to be men. Men still largely have the power and control, and make the decisions.
- Most women seem to be clustered at the lower end of the hierarchy. Women tend not to have power or control, or make decisions.
- In certain occupations – usually the most powerful and prestigious – women are scarcely represented, and in others – generally lower in pay and status – they abound.

We could go further, and jump to another set of conclusions – highly disturbing, some of them, but consistent with the statistics.

- Women can't get power.
- Women can't handle power.
- Many organisations are not operating the legal machinery properly.
- Existing legal machinery is useless.
- Men are keeping women out and down without contravening the law.
- Women are better at serving and caring than leading and directing.
- Many jobs are unsuitable for women.
- Some jobs are unsuitable for men.
- There are men's ways of working, and women's ways of working. They don't match, and are better kept apart.
- The workplace is not an environment where women thrive.
- Only extraordinary women can match average men.
- There are more extraordinary men than women.
- Women get things wrong.
- Women don't have the guts or skill to rise above the average.
- The best man wins every time.
- Women don't want to be at the top.
- Women are doing something they think is more important, outside the workplace.

Such conclusions underlie the dialogue of defensiveness and protest that can be heard every day between men and women working together. Overheard snatches from that dialogue . . .

'If she can't stand the heat she should get out of the kitchen.'
'Men don't listen, and they won't let you get a word in edgeways.'
'He's so patronising.'

'When things go wrong she blames everyone but herself.'
'He thinks because I'm blonde I must be stupid.'
'He keeps putting his arm round me and I don't know what to say.'
'Her expectations are totally unrealistic.'
'He never makes the tea.'
'She's not committed to work the way a man would be.'
'If I go into his room I stand and wait for him to attend me – if he comes into mine he just bursts in and takes over.'
'She takes things so personally.'
'He looked just like a little boy who'd broken his toy.'
'She's a bit of all right, know what I mean.'
'He puts me down all the time.'
'I don't know what she's on about. It's just the same for men.'
'She's a real bitch – so aggressive.'
'He's gorgeous.'
'Anyway, I often make the tea.'
'He said we'd do the conference together but all I did was hand him the slides.'
'Why are women so sensitive about things that aren't important?'
'He expects me to look after him.'
'We'd like a woman in the job, but we haven't found one with the right personality.'
'He won't take me seriously.'

Of course men and women say positive things about one another, too. Not everybody is dissatisfied with the way things are. And of course the things people say depend on their age, their experience and their own personality. But on both sides of the dialogue there's a powerful undercurrent of negative reactions to working with members of the opposite sex. Many of these are based not on the party line, but on observation of actual behaviour at work, or what's let slip in the heat of the moment. Here's an example: the cautionary tale of a group of men and women who had been working amicably and quite productively together for some time. They felt they were not as effective as they might be, and so they decided to polish up their teamwork by spending a couple of days on an outdoor management development programme, run by Training in Action of Truro.

The moment arrived when one of the men and the three women were at the top of a cliff with a rope, and the other three men were at the bottom. The three at the bottom called to the four at the top to haul up a load of planks, and the man yelled back: 'I can't – there's nobody here but me!'

All hell broke loose. Shock, fury, incredulity, incomprehension, bitter recriminations, self-defence.

What the man said was insensitive and tactless. What he meant (so he said) was: 'This is a job which depends on qualities which I have and these women do not. I must therefore take personal responsibility, for the benefit of the whole team.' What the women heard was: 'Women don't count. They can't contribute to this activity. No need to discuss it – I've made the decision.' The offender would say he accepted without argument that women deserve equal opportunities, and should be judged on merit. However, when the chips were down, he behaved like a throwback who'd never considered these propositions.

The fallout began painfully and outlasted the training course. It led eventually to a useful development of relationships and a more effective team. Catch people unawares, and by highlighting the gap between what they say and how they behave, you can identify the material on which to build more honest relationships.

Comments which might have been heard as a matter of course in the workplace twenty years ago still crop up – but rarely, sheepishly and obliquely. It's not done to suggest that men are brighter than women, or that there are occupations unfit for women, or that a woman's place is in the home. Less often do people say categorically: 'I could never work for a woman,' or accuse women of taking the bread out of men's mouths by filling jobs which are rightfully theirs. It would be terrific to think that these are ghosts which have been well and truly laid. We may imagine, because we mostly hear the right words and not the wrong ones, that we are further away from the bad old days than we really are. However, there is a time-lag: what we think and what we do tend to trail behind what we say. There is no guarantee that, because the words are not spoken, the prejudices don't exist. Facts, behaviour and private opinions often contradict what people say when they're supporting 'politically correct' standpoints. Sincerity becomes suspect and faith is in short supply.

There are plenty of men who say that women are not only

welcome, but necessary in the workplace. Men have, they feel, already embraced the inevitability of more power and influence for women, and are even prepared to accept that this is not magnanimity but self-interest – and that their forebears got it wrong. But many women reinterpret that view with a certain amount of cynicism. They think it is a plan for damage limitation, and that men are carefully controlling the power they can afford to give away before they lose what they really value. Women think men are only handing over the areas they don't want. Women are welcome, in their place, at lower levels, where they can be coped with, on men's terms, with a touch of smug thuggery.

Men feel they are on a hiding to nothing. If they don't say clearly that they value women, they are labelled sexist. If they do, women retort that they are being patronising and patriarchal. Men may say – they maintain quite genuinely – that they think women are wonderful. And look what they get in return: ingratitude and resentment. If a top man says how proud he is that over three-quarters of his workforce is female, women picture some enormous henhouse, with all the women scratching about after each other, and looking up to the ultimate authority with obedience. Cock-a-doodle-doo.

Men think that the changes women want are within women's power to make. Women feel as though they are constantly coming up against barriers erected by men. When women describe these obstacles, men find it hard to believe they are there. Frustration meets bafflement.

## *The trigger of the Nineties*

People of both sexes may be tempted to shrug, sit back, and think: well, what the hell? We've tottered along so far and we seem to have done OK. Such an attitude would be irresponsible and shortsighted even if today's organisations were going to move into the foreseeable future in much the same shape and style as they currently display. But they aren't – and the things that are predicted to happen in the next ten or twenty years make it even more imperative that we address the issues now.

- **For personal and economic reasons, women want and need to work.**
Women are crying out to get into the job market. Their cries are loud, if largely unorchestrated, and they fall into three main categories.

*Women want jobs badly because they need the money badly.*
Often we act as though the workplace only had to cater for the old traditional concept of 'the breadwinner and his wife', as though the nuclear family of forty years ago were still in universal existence, as though women still have the option of earning pin-money for the little luxuries of life, and workers (men) can rely on full-time domestic support. But, in fact, only 7 or 8 per cent of the 19.5 million households in Britain still comprise a husband who works and a wife who stays at home with the children – down from 12 per cent in 1979. One-parent households are increasing. For many people, men or women, there simply is no choice. They have to work – or go under. And women require work which exceeds the very basic, ill-paid, part-time options which are often all that's available.

*Work promises a level of self-development women can't get elsewhere.*
There's a limit to the personal growth you an experience as you slave over hot stove and crappy nappies. The 'private life' of women has its pleasures and challenges – but they tend to be repetitive and unsung. Women are conscious of their own spare capacity, skills going begging, and a deep curiosity to know how far they can get. They are experts at adding value to what they do at home. But there's potential for excitement, involvement, creativity on a bigger scale outside. Many women want to be rats racing.

*Women want to work because they can.*
It's a challenge they are ready to rise to. The Everest factor – climb it because it's there. Enough of a precedent has been set by enough pioneering women to create work opportunies which no longer present wild frontiers to conquer. Moral support for 'working mothers' is not universal, but it is increasing. It's more common for women to regard their jobs as lifetime careers, not as interludes of money-making to supplement the family income. We haven't quite got to the stage where women take it for granted, as men do, that they will have to earn their living all their life. In times of high unemployment, they certainly don't even take it for granted that they can get a job. But if there's a chance, many of them will grab it.

- **And, just as much as women need the workplace, the workplace needs women.**
*The birth slump in the Seventies has left organisations with the prospect of a decade or so in which they will be short of traditional sources of skills, hands and brains.*
Women have historically become a precious resource when there is no other option. In 1989 the Government predicted that by the year 2000 the number of people in the workforce aged under 25 would have fallen by up to a third, which would leave gaping holes in organisations where skilled professionals, managers and operatives used to be. Yet organisations have been desperately slow in preparing for a shortage of young talent which has been on the cards for a decade. They were saved – if that's the word – only by the recession. Who needs to harness an under-utilised resource when the market-place is seething with experienced workers, professionals and managers who have been let go and are only too keen to be let back in again? However, the underlying demographic trend remains; and many organisations seem intent on muddling through. The risk is that they will be in real trouble when the recovery comes, because the small fund of young employees from traditional sources will be spread too thinly to service them all.

Companies will have to compete for women, not only against others in the same boat, but also against the attraction of self-employment. Rather than wait – impatiently and perhaps in vain – for established organisations to come up with the goods, many women are going it alone and taking the entrepreneurial route to self-fulfilment. The number of businesses owned by women has doubled in Europe over the last ten years.

According to the 1990 Hansard Society Commission report *Women at the Top*: 'Companies which adopt and publicise management development practices that benefit women's careers will have a distinct advantage in recruitment and gain an important edge over their competitors.'

*At the same time Britain is part of the single European market, which faces tougher competition worldwide.*
The single market has spiced up the competition. There are more organisations requiring a high-calibre workforce, and a bigger pool of potential employees. Joanna Foster, president of the EC's Advisory Committee on Equal Opportunities: 'The strongest country will be the one that has invested in a quality workforce. And half of those are women.'

*Organisations are changing profoundly.*
Organisations are under pressure to change rapidly and fundamentally. They have found that some of the old methods of doing things are way out of date. Standing still is a recipe for being left behind. New factors rocket in from the outside; but even if they didn't, the progressive organisation constantly reviews its own mission and purpose, and the methods it employs to achieve them, in order to stay ahead of the game and maintain its competitive advantage. Demands are being generated for diverse skills, a talent for flexibility, a touch of empathy for colleagues and customers – benefits which are comparatively rare at present, but which are classically associated with women.

We have failed in the objectives of twenty years ago. The dearth of women at higher levels and in certain areas is absurd. It's clearly not enough to rely on legal machinery. Government tends to be all mouth and no skirts. It hasn't secured a more sensibly balanced two-sex workplace in the last twenty years, and it's not likely to in the next twenty.

There's strong evidence that we have failed to change attitudes, too. In the day-to-day working environment – beyond law and money and politics – the quality of the relations betwen the sexes is something between an irritant and a disaster. At worst, there is overall discomfort and overt conflict. At best, negative feelings may be sloshing about under the surface – unfinished business not directly connected with the objectives of the organisation, never properly addressed and constantly clouding effective performance of the task. Organisational indigestion with the occasional pang of heartburn. Or, more threatening, buckets of bile and searing pain.

At the same time, compelling commercial arguments point to the crucial and increasing importance of what women can offer to the workplace. Women themselves are eager to contribute. Something needs to be done.

To have a hope of sorting out what this should be, we need to pay much closer attention to the detail of daily working activities. How effectively are women and men working together, *now*?

# 2 How the Other Half Work

**Q:** *Do men and women work the same way, or are they different?*
**A:** *Yes.*

Let us start by setting out, very briefly, a broad context for comparing men and women, before narrowing the focus to the work arena and examining some aspects of apparent difference in more detail.

We use stereotypes to make sense of the environment. Patterns which seem to fit whole groups of people provide us with a shortcut to help us predict their likely behaviour, and select the most appropriate behaviour for ourselves. Most of us have fixed ideas about men and women. As with most stereotypes, they are likely to contain a good deal of truth, and much misleading garbage – and it's often hard to tell which. As John Nicholson points out in his book *Men and Women: How Different Are They?* countless studies have examined boys and girls, men and women, identical and fraternal twins, people with ordinary and extraordinary chromosomes, in an attempt to unpack sex stereotypes, isolate real, observable differences, and attribute them to some identifiable source.

There are major difficulties in trying to tie down sex differences. Life would be nice and neat if we could confidently assert that any difference we can detect is substantial; that the differences are split right down the middle, with all the men on one side and all the women on the other; and that the chromosomes which mark them out as men and women are totally responsible for the difference.

Unfortunately, none of these things can be done. For one thing, research measures are often too crude. There are too many variables, apart from sex. And you can't look solely to biology to account for any difference you do detect, because it is so confounded with upbringing, social conditioning and expectation.

What emerges from the research is that chromosomes may dictate the shape of our genitals, but they certainly aren't enough alone to account for gender differences in our behaviour. For instance, from a baby's birth parental expectation can create habits of response which mould both baby and parents. If a baby girl cries, the parents' response is often that she is upset and needs to be soothed and comforted. If a baby boy cries, he is often treated as though he were bored and frustrated, and is therefore given new stimulation, and encouraged to be active and adventurous. Baby girls smile more than baby boys – and parents respond by talking to them and encouraging them to be sociable – which inspires baby girls to smile more. Small biological differences become magnified by experience and treatment, so that boys and girls tread along divergent paths. The differences are encapsulated in exaggerated stereotypes which influence behaviour and proceed to perpetuate themselves.

The question of gender is part of the bigger question of identity which exercises each of us from the moment of conception – and never stops. As children grow up and their observation and understanding sharpen, their view of men and women changes. As toddlers they have no particular expectation of what a Mummy or Daddy should be like. Thereafter they pass through a succession of stages. At one point they are convinced that biology is destiny, and men and women behave as they do because they are made that way. At another they begin to understand that individuals' personalities make a difference. They learn to see the wider influence of the social system on the people they know. In pursuit of their own place in this framework they pass through a phase of clinging to the parameters set for their own sex-role stereotype, and then learn to relax the rules as they become more confident of their identity. At each stage, friends and teachers reward and reinforce some kinds of behaviour and criticise others, according to the value they attribute to it and whether it is thought appropriate to the child's biological sex. For instance, boys learn to be tough, and to hide fear; girls learn to care for others, and that they can show fear but not anger. Bravery is highly esteemed, and boys are expected to display more of it than girls. The significance an adult attaches to masculinity or femininity depends on the way in which that individual has learned to interpret them during the progress of their development, under the influence of the prevailing culture.

It's more of a struggle for boys to achieve their sense of identity than for girls. They need to feel strongly differentiated from their womenfolk in order to achieve a clear identity of their own. Boys will be boys? Yes – provided that they do what males do and not what females do – and they have to work hard at it. While small girls watch and listen and take turns, small boys take up time and space with uproarious activity in which they compete and fight and pursue their individual agendas.

This would be interesting enough if the distinctions created between the sexes by the stereotypes portrayed only *difference*. In fact, the stereotypes also represent *value judgments*. From early on in life, a higher value is attributed to what males do – and this is as true in most other cultures as in our own. Little boys who act like girls attract ridicule and contempt, while little girls who act like boys are more likely to elicit admiration. Teachers – often unwittingly – give boys more time and attention. John Nicholson quotes research which shows that British schoolchildren are more disrespectful of female teachers than males, and that boys work harder for male teachers. When respondents are asked to complete questionnaires about sex-role stereotypes by applying adjectives to the appropriate gender and stating whether they are positive or negative attributes, men get far more of the positive ones.

If the culture is one in which masculine behaviour and attitudes are paramount, unravelling gender stereotypes, whether by scientists or ordinary people, becomes very problematical. The obvious thing to do is to define women's behaviour and attitudes in masculine terms. As Dale Spender makes clear in her book *Man Made Language*, research itself can become misdirected and indeed biased, because it is based on masculine norms. She was speaking of language research, but it's just as true of studies in other areas. Early research into work practices was largely based on men, but findings were presented as if they were universally applicable. If women's results are shown to be different from men's the difference is often expressed as a deficiency on women's part, or a vagary which can be ignored. Questions relevant to women may not be represented in research results. They may not even have been asked, because they are not recognised as significant in a man's world.

When it comes to 'working people', unpacking stereotypes is just as difficult – and relying on them just as tempting. As one banker said, ruefully: 'I know sex stereotypes are limiting and dangerous. I don't fit the stereotype of "working women" all that neatly myself – but, even knowing that, I have to make a big effort not to be prejudiced by received ideas about women and men when customers come to ask for a business loan.' It is hard to jettison received ideas. Stereotyped pen-pictures of men and women in the workplace are readily compiled.

> **Men.** Men operate by power and control. Their universe is held together by their sense of hierarchy. The only difference between people that matters is: who's winning? Competition is vital; men want to be winners. A clear sense of who is one-up and where they stand increases masculine comfort, so if a contest doesn't exist, men may need to invent one. Action and achievement mark progress. Size of pay-packet is a crucial bench-mark of success, so money is of enormous interest. Men are confident beings. They may be aggressive, but softer emotions are not important to them. Men talk about facts, actions, abstract ideas, the big picture. They don't listen much. Dominance is their chief goal; failure is their chief fear.

> **Women.** Women operate by creating links with other people. Their universe is held together by a network of relationships. They want to minimise status differences between themselves and others, so that they can optimise the chance of sharing experiences, and form a sense of being part of an overall community, in which everyone has a different contribution to make. They seek intimacy and involvement with other people, which implies they certainly don't want to fight them. Women are interested in feelings, people, relationships, detail. Listening is one of their principal skills. They lack confidence.

Their emotions are close to the surface. Interdependence is
their chief goal; isolation is their chief fear.

'Not me, not me!' I hear you cry. Is there any truth in these
portrayals? Well, yes and no. Saville and Holdsworth Ltd, the well-
known company of occupational psychologists, produce a widely
used series of Occupational Personality Questionnaires which get
people to rate themselves on various aspects of personality. In 1991
Saville and Holdsworth compiled a standardisation study based on
1365 men and 1567 women, two-thirds of them 'working', a sample
targeted to be representative of the national population in terms of
age spread, gender and socio-economic grouping. The study provides a snapshot which outlines – for one moment in time – the
effects of age and gender on responses to the questionnaire. We
can't assume that responses by forty-year-olds now are typical of
responses which will always be made by forty-year-olds. However,
the results overall are quite close to the stereotype. Men see
themselves as more controlling than women at all ages, and the sex
difference is biggest in the late forties. This may not be a factor of
age at all, but a result of the very different parental expectations
and upbringing of boys and girls born in the 1940s and '50s.
Women generally see themselves as more consultative. One of the
biggest sex differences in the whole study is that women are more
interested in the welfare of others at all ages. But the older they
get, the more caring men become. Men are interested in working
with their hands, and in numbers and data; women prefer culture,
the arts, and what makes people tick. Men think they have more
ideas than women. There is little difference in conscientiousness or
attention to detail. Men are more relaxed: women worry much
more than men, especially from their mid-thirties onwards. A
major sex difference is that men think they are much more
toughminded, thickskinned, and difficult to hurt. They also see
themselves as much more competitive, becoming less so as they get
older.

Nevertheless, the differences between the sexes are minor. Dr
George Sik of Saville and Holdsworth likens the research results to
the caption on the old seaside postcard: 'There are no big differences between women and men – but some of the small ones are

*very* interesting.' The range of differences between women at extremes or men at extremes is much greater than those between the average woman and the average man. A tough, confident man would be very like a tough, confident woman, and very unlike a gentle, timid man. Of course, people answering questions about themselves may have in mind benchmarks specific to their own gender, so that, for instance, when women rate themselves 'very confident' they may mean 'very confident – for a woman'. Other research suggests that men and women working in organisations are even more alike than men and women outside it. Chickens and eggs: do men and women with similar profiles go into organisations, or does being in the workplace give them similar profiles? There's no easy way to tell, but the net result, at least, is that members of both sexes can display the whole range of behaviours, both 'masculine' and 'feminine'.

It seems that men and women do see some truth in the stereotypes – but there's also a big overlap between them, so we can't rely on them to help us predict individual reactions. And, as the banker recognised, they are dangerous. All too often, stereotypes are used as prescriptions or verdicts. 'This is how men ought to be', or 'This is how women are'. Because the workplace is a man's world, the masculine stereotype is the one that seems to fit best with the received view of how a 'worker' should be. Men and women are not as different as they sometimes think they are, but their beliefs about their own sex and the opposite one, and the value ascribed to each, create discrepancies when they interact.

The difference is really caused by emphasis. Men and women may attach a different weight and priority to the behaviours they share. Women do know how to compete, and men do know how to co-operate; women can argue, and men can listen attentively; it's just not their first choice of behaviour, on the whole, and a lot depends on context. Get men and women together, and they all know what they are talking about; but they often disagree on the slant they bring to the situation, and what should be done about it. The change of emphasis increases the apparent gap, and makes the differences look more significant and more extreme. Therefore the way women and men respond to events and each other can produce hiccups in the smooth running of working practice, day by day.

Examples of some of the potential mismatches follow. We take a look at a selection of the areas where the biggest contrasts between the sex stereotypes seem to occur: confidence and assertiveness, aggression and competition, and feelings.

## Confidence

The biggest difference between me and the men I meet at work is one of confidence. They seem to have it, I don't. Its absence is also the biggest similarity between me and many of the women I meet. A sex difference in confidence is visible very early in children's lives, and it stalks the research findings like a fiend.

Confidence is closely linked to a sense of control, which develops differently for girls and boys. During their development, boys tend to have more opportunities for exercising control, and more encouragement to do so, than girls. Parents usually protect girls from the outside world more strictly than boys. Anxiety about boys centres on traffic accidents, and about girls on the possibility of attack or sexual assault. One study showed that by the time children were seven there was a marked difference between the levels of adult surveillance boys and girls could expect, and that this sex difference persisted as they grew older. Another factor in controlling the environment is the presence of role-models. In my youth children's stories, films and television programmes had boys as heroes and girls as onlookers and purveyors of picnics. They did not inspire girls to believe they could naturally make things happen. The balance is being redressed, but some studies suggest that simply showing males and females in non-stereotyped roles does not automatically reverse tradition: children, like adults, often selectively attend to the characters and situations which fit best with the ideas they already hold about gender roles. Parents, too, are powerful role-models; again patterns have changed in the last twenty years, but it takes time for beliefs held by previous generations to become modified. Many women of my mother's generation still talk as though women can't possibly be competent in any sphere where men also exist, and if they make any claims to competence they should do it rather quietly in a backwater. Some of her generation passed on to some of mine a sense that what women do lacks value, and I have a nagging feeling that, if my sons had been daughters, I'd have transferred it down the line. One way and another, it is easier for girls to learn to be helpless. By the time they reach young adulthood, women are less likely then men to believe they can control their environment – and more likely to show lower levels of confidence.

Many women launch themselves into a circular, self-destructive pattern of self-doubt, based on acceptance of masculine definitions of worth. Research suggests that women don't undervalue their skills or their talents, and feel that they compare very favourably with those of men – but that they are much less confident than men that they can achieve their aims. They accept the merit of men's contribution at face value, and at the same time focus more on their own shortfalls. Women pick up a clear set of lessons. Don't be bold, be safe. Don't give anything one hundred per cent *in public*, because it is not good enough. Don't put your head over the parapet, because it will expose your undoubted ineffectiveness.

Women tend, so research suggests, to have a lower opinion of other women than of men, and it is sometimes lower than the opinion men hold of women. When the first woman weather forecaster appeared on British television, a study of the audience response showed that men rated male and female forecasters equally, but women were harder on the female. Faced with evidence that women can do it – whatever it is – women fight hard not to accept it. The logic, if that's what you call it, seems to go something like this:

> I am a woman, and I doubt that I will achieve much. All around me I see men being competent and authoritative. Therefore other women must really be incompetent and insufficient. It's OK for women to step into the breach in times of crisis, because that must be better than nothing. Anything good that women achieve is a fluke, unsustainable, special; kept on a shelf, as it were, as a one-off in case of emergency; probably not a repeatable phenomenon; probably a faint copy of something a man would have done better. It's safer to rely on sustainable authority from men.

When they meet uncertainty or opposition women are less likely to become angry and forceful than depressed and self-critical – or, as one senior manager put it: 'Women are hand-wringers, not neck-wringers.' Given that by many masculine criteria women fall short all the time, perpetual self-doubt is an understandable viewpoint – but it leads nowhere but down, and ways have to be found to interrupt the spiral.

Men learn different lessons. According to the research, little boys consistently over-estimate their influence on their surroundings, their importance to others, what they believe they can achieve in future, and their own share of the credit when things go well. Their upbringing helps them acquire the habit of maintaining control, and men have greater faith than women in their ability to do so. If they meet failure they shrug it off, where a woman might wallow in it; they ignore adverse comment; they deny anything which threatens self-belief, having learned to act as though it did not exist. They are the Great Pretenders.

I asked many men and women what they do when they doubt their capacity. The women displayed different levels of confidence in themselves, but none of them was under any illusion about what I meant by the question. Many of the men, on the other hand, found it difficult to give a direct response. 'You don't seem to understand,' said one man. 'It's not that men are acting, or papering over the cracks – we don't *have* any doubts.' Magnificent. Or blinkered, complacent and arrogant.

Some men did admit insecurities, but they were limited. One common reaction from men to descriptions of how things are for women was: 'Well, that's no different for men.' The Chairman of one large company said: 'Men are worried about meeting strangers and walking into bars on their own, too.' Sometimes insecurity must be worse, because there is an expectation of what men should live up to which not every man can fulfil. But men have learned to act with confidence, which is the first step towards having it.

What women describe is on a different plane altogether from natural nervousness about certain situations. It's not temporary stage-fright, but a kitbag of troubles which women take with them. Women who fear – with however little justification – that they can't match up to the demands of work, may nevertheless try to behave as though they are successfully meeting them. They then feel they must be imposters deceiving the world. One thirty-seven-year-old woman talked herself into a highly-paid job after an early career as a typist, and fifteen years as a housewife and mother of four. 'I felt a total fraud. I kept expecting a tap on the shoulder – 'Hey, what do you think you're doing here?' – but eventually I realised it was a piece of cake. I couldn't believe how easy it was.' She came to terms early with the fact that what she was doing was equal in standard to what she said she was doing – and she needed that level of self-belief to keep up the quality of her performance. But there are highly-respected and established women who should be basking in their success, yet who feel that it's all a sham – that what they are purporting to offer cannot possibly be justified. One such woman – a journalist – said: 'I'm still frightened of being found out. I spin out the little I have.'

I asked Paul Brack, Assistant Director of Finance at Croydon Borough Council, how he would describe men in situations where they were unsure of themselves. He said: 'The motto would be something like "Oh, sod it – give it a go!" They'd pretend they had the knowledge; talk with strong confidence as if they had it, to people who don't have the detail. Make mistakes look less disastrous than they are so that they protect their image. The idea is to get away with it. I suppose we bottle up anxiety, find a strong opinion and push.' He felt that the key to confidence was the building of a powerbase of information. He agreed that women need more shoring up than men, on the whole: 'Sometimes,' he said, 'you have to make an effort to convince a woman she's worth it, that she *can* handle the job.'

For women, the knowledge of effort and hard work behind an achievement may justify it. Women are desperately conscientious. The Principal of St Hilda's College, Oxford, says that it's still the women who write down all the lecture notes and faithfully use them to back up their examination essays. But it doesn't necessarily give them what she calls the Alpha Touch. Men take the risk of being less conscientious, and get proportionately more first-class degrees. ('You know why,' said one cynic. 'They borrow their girlfriends' notes!') If it isn't hard work, women feel it's of questionable validity. When a male colleague and I ran workshops together, he was impatient with my anxiety and earnestness. 'It doesn't have to be hard to be good,' said he, all the time. Effort should be followed by achievement – but for women, even that doesn't always feel deserved unless there's some pain in it somewhere. A young female barrister sees women as being handicapped by their very clarity of vision. 'Women lay themselves open to more difficulties – they don't have a level of confidence and optimism. Men are cocky. They're not better, or stronger, or more able – they're just blind to the problems they're up against. They don't see the pitfalls. It would be great to be oblivious. I know very few cocky women.' It may be blindness that contributes to the success of many men. If there are problems they can't deal with, they discount them. Perhaps men have had responses to fear knocked out of them: hiding fear works better. So, like the Incredible Hulk, they walk through obstacles as if they weren't there – and this gains them the plaudits they require.

Men don't talk about gratitude, and women do. If you can't believe you have the right to be there, then you must owe somebody something. Nothing can safely be put down to just deserts – not even your job. Where men speak of needing to earn their living, taking it for granted that they will be the breadwinner, women are much more likely to question their right to be in the workplace, their level of contribution, and the terms on which they are accepted. One woman solicitor, while talking of her experiences at work, said: 'I'm pathetically grateful for the flexibility . . . I'm pathetically grateful to my colleagues . . .' Thank you, someone, somewhere, for letting me be where I am, doing what I'm doing. Ignore the fact that I may have earned the right all by myself. Gratitude is a gracious thing to feel when there is reason for it, but crippling when there isn't. Gratitude may imply some sort of inequality in the transaction. 'I'm a second-class citizen – there by grace and favour,' said a middle manager in a distribution company. Women should learn to take a bit more for granted.

If you are not confident in what you are and what you offer, then it becomes harder to make demands, too. Women don't like to take up too much of people's time and attention. Even little boys at school have been shown to take far more of their teachers' time than girls. One Royal Mail Customer Care Manager had to learn a new set of skills and information rather quickly when Royal Mail was organised in early 1992. Male colleagues said, quite naturally: 'Well, ring up a few people and ask.' 'Oh, I couldn't,' she said. 'Why should they help me? I've got nothing to offer them. I feel awkward about asking for anything when I can't give something back in return.' Her colleagues thought she was being silly. They couldn't understand why she was making such a fuss about a simple activity. I told her about the Banque Centrale – the hypothetical psychological bank of good deeds. You make deposits when you have the wherewithal and withdrawals when you need them. Some central providence ensures the funds are allocated where appropriate, and so you needn't feel you have had more than you deserve. This convinced her she was entitled to ask. Men are more likely to assume their entitlement and go for what they want.

Even if they can accept that they deserve the success they have achieved, another thing females learn early is not to mention it. I'm a highly educated woman, and I'm proud of my academic successes, but only in private. Degrees are at least some measure of credibility, but I have found myself being totally, unreasonably defensive about them if they're mentioned in public. I fought (and failed) to leave them off my business cards, so as not to be exposed as the bluestocking and brainbox people used to hate me for being, back in 1966 when I got my O-Level results. For men qualifications add status; for women they can reduce popularity. One American study asked High School teachers and students to judge the intelligence, personality and adjustment of a very successful hypothetical student, who was presented as modest or immodest about their achievements. The least popular was the immodest female, and a modest female was judged more popular that a modest male. If success can bring you rejection or disapproval, and these are important to you, then you have two choices: don't have any successes, or have them and keep quiet.

If modesty stops women blowing trumpets, they can be tempted to resent men as conceited because they do list their achievements and get themselves noticed. 'Women don't do enough PR for themselves,' said an Oxford psychologist, ruefully. 'I only go to one conference to tell the world about the discoveries I've made, not to five – like men do – to tell everybody how clever I've been.'

It may be a misperception on women's part; it's not necessarily true that self-aggrandisement is men's prime motivation. They may be using all possible means to circulate vital information. Women who are not sure about their right to speak up properly don't test it by drawing attention to themselves unless thay have to; and it's easy to overlook the fact that sometimes it is a requirement of the job. 'At the weekly conference I don't say anything because I don't know anything,' said a woman journalist. There she is, doing the job – and yet, in some topsy-turvy fashion, she remains unconvinced that this gives her either the right or the responsibility to contribute. One school of thought suggests that women of the generation after mine are less hamstrung. However, I've been surprised when listening to women in their twenties to find many of them still quite tentative. When Rosemary Thorne was appointed as Sainsbury's first female Finance Director in March 1992, she was quoted in the *Daily Telegraph* as saying that speaking up was a basic principle of success in finance. 'Younger women often tend to be quiet and reserved. You shouldn't be frightened to make a noise – not necessarily about gender issues, but about anything relating to the business. Females are brought up to be more subservient than men, and particularly at the start of your career it's a disadvantage to be too quiet.'

Lower levels of confidence seem to be more widespread amongst women, to start earlier in life, and to be fatally easy to teach. Men say: 'I believe.' Women say: 'I think.' The weakness of the woman's response is that it admits self-doubt and carries less conviction, so that she presents potential critics with a foothold for opposition. The weakness of the man's response is that he diminishes opportunities for learning, by shutting out any invitation to provide alternatives. But the male response is much more acceptable. Men need to re-evaluate their own behaviour in order to ensure that the conviction they express is based on more than complacency and forcefulness.

Being frightened of rejection by other people, not being sure you have permission to have convictions, not having the courage to believe in them, and not being able to say what successes you have achieved, can only be a recipe for disaster. It's enough to stop many women getting into the workplace, or into the higher reaches of it, where they may be tested to destruction. Many top managers say they would be delighted to offer senior jobs to women – but they can't unless women apply for them, and they don't. Sights may be set low by women because setting them high invites pain.

Women themselves need to do something about this: to push themselves out of their comfort zone, stick their necks out and pay the price, if necessary, in guilt and gratitude – and then teach their daughters to do it without cost. The impetus must come from women. But that impetus needs to be matched by an environment in which it is understood and encouraged, and where allowances are made for the difficulties in pursuing it. Women need support from colleagues. Some men understand this. A very senior Director explained why he'd badgered a female colleague into a role she thought beyond her. 'She wanted to do it – and she didn't want to do it. So I nagged her, and she did it.'

Margaret Beckett, Deputy Leader of the Labour Party said in a *Sunday Times* interview on 19 January 1992: 'Like most women, if people hadn't pushed me, I wouldn't have done it. All through my political career there has been someone who has said to me, "Why don't you stand for that?" If I'd had to step forward and say, "I want to do that", I wouldn't be here now.' Women need invitations and reassurance, not just opportunities.

Confidence brings assertiveness. Assertiveness is the key to making things happen. Men don't, on the whole, get offered assertiveness training. Assertiveness is assumed to be a 'natural' part of the masculine package – the positive face of aggression. For many men, it's easy to believe that women who learn to be assertive are threatening; they are afraid women will start behaving like men – confronting others, but with all the unpredictability of women. 'Send 'em off to be trained, and they'll come back saying "No, damn you!" and telling you where to go.' The pattern is confusing even to women. One female Detective-Constable said: 'How do you define the line of how to stay a lady? I want to remain a woman and not turn into a hard, tough bitch.' She apparently shares some men's evaluation: women who purposefully aim to get what they want or need are unfeminine.

Most assertiveness training aims to help women compensate for their 'natural' tendency to hang back. But it's also about how to make things happen *without betraying gender*: how to combat the stereotype of woman as powerless wimp, but still look and sound like a woman. It's not that women lack the capacity to be assertive; it's a choice they make, because they are afraid that if they shape events firmly they will hurt people's feelings, seem negative, be punished, look bossy. Women feel taking a back seat makes them seem more like team players, gives them a better chance of gaining friends, helps them fulfil all conceivable obligations, and still maintain their femininity. Training courses offer new techniques for action which don't try to turn women into pseudo-men: behaviour which is acceptable and credible, not only to workmates, but to women themselves. Women can learn how to accept constructive criticism gracefully, instead of taking it personally; how to be more direct; how to stop emotions taking over; how to say no without feeling guilty; how to handle difficult people and awkward situations while maintaining respect.

Learning how to be assertive is fine provided women know what they are to be assertive *about*. They can learn to say a firm: 'No, thank you,' without beating around the bush and stammering out justifications; but it's no earthly good if they're agonising over whether they have the right to refuse in the first place. They need more than a form of words. Women need to know what they want, believe both that they have the right to try to get it and that they will have enough strength themselves and support from others to surmount the obstacles. Building up a credit reserve of confidence in themselves is women's task, but in the face of negative reactions from others the effort of being assertive can push them into spiritual overdraft. It's useful for women to understand techniques, but not in a vacuum. Interaction with men is part of it all. Women need to learn to feel better about taking responsibility for making things happen. Men have to understand exactly why women feel bad about it in the first place, and accept that admitting alternative points of view can have positive results. Both men and women need insights, not only into the behaviour of the opposite sex, but into their own.

## Aggression and competition

Working life can be viewed as some kind of sublimation of all the exciting and adventurous things men have ever been: warriors, gangsters, cowboys and Indians, pirates, musketeers, explorers, cops and robbers. Adventures depend on a contest between individuals or groups, or between an individual and the environment, which one party has to win by displaying dominance, and which culminates in the collection of a reward.

Whereas careers followed mainly by women focus on help and support for others, those which men pursue often seem to require an element of aggressiveness: an understanding of how to deliver it and how to take it like a man, on the chin. But it's a myth that only men can be aggressive. True, physical violence remains largely the domain of men. However, although studies of aggression do not give a consistent picture, research suggests that, although men are more likely to knock people about physically, women are just as likely to use aggression that causes psychological harm. Men are believed to be more aggressive than women, and so they are; but women are also often seen to foment male aggression. Sex differences in aggression are small, and becoming smaller. Women may have been taught that anger and aggression are unladylike, but it doesn't always stop them behaving aggressively.

Aggression is not necessarily valued by Real Men. I talked to an ex-brigadier and an ex-colonel who had both gone into industry. Both said that, although the difference between military and civilian existence was enormous, even in the highly masculine Army you make things happen by persuading people, not by pushing their faces in. However, whatever they say about it, men do use aggression in the workplace. Sometimes it is the next step on from displaying control and dominance. Aggression tends to be the resort of men when the chips are down and they are facing apparently intractable opposition; or when they are presented with a situation which they find frightening or hard to comprehend; or when they are acting single-mindedly to achieve a result without considering other parties involved. It's a way of ploughing through an obstacle without exploring it; being a Big Battalion that God is on the side of.

It may look like aggression from the outside, but to men it often doesn't feel like aggression from the inside, and they are surprised when it is brought home to them. Videos of participants at training workshops give them a first-class opportunity to explore any differences between the message they thought they sent and the message which was received. A man may, for instance, go through a counselling role-play. Afterwards, the comments made by his colleagues in the audience are so critical that he simply doesn't believe them. Then he watches himself on video. What he thought was masterly guidance of a dialogue is revealed as a one-sided contest, a power-play. Very often, he's horrified to find that what comes out on video is a whole lot louder and more confrontational than it felt at the time. He sees in action replay what he didn't notice live. There is the interviewee, tense, monosyllabic, shuffling feet. There is the interviewer – himself, leaning forward across the barrier of a table to invade the interviewee's space, jutting his chin forward, interrupting, showing little expression, greeting information with disbelief or disapproval. He only meant to keep control, and to test things out, probe and challenge – and quite right too – but it came over as aggression because he didn't read or react to the response, and didn't gauge his own impact on the other party.

Competition is what men are born for, says the stereotype, and this can lead men to translate situations into contests in a way which women often find hard to take. Results of research into competition are not cut and dried. It is clear that both men and women are motivated to achieve something worthwhile. Some research among boys and girls suggests that competition motivates boys more than girls – but that it only brings them to the level of motivation which girls experience without it. Another suggestion is that many men compete intensely because they are afraid of being losers; women less strongly because they are afraid that if they win their relationship with the loser will be damaged. Other research emphasises the fact that competitive and co-operative activity do not take place in a vacuum, and strategies observed may have been prompted by a range of motives. For instance, a co-operative move may have been taken to maximise an individual's reward, or in total disregard of the available reward, with the sole aim of helping the other party. A competitive tactic may have been prompted by the desire either to win a reward, or to vanquish an opponent. The results of many experimental studies suggest that the gender of players' opponents has more impact on their strategy than their own gender. Men are more competitive with other men and all strong players; women are more competitive with weaker opponents. This leads to a complex choice for men and women, as women join the workplace in new areas. The stereotype suggests that women are weak and compliant, men strong and dominant. Men expect to fight the strong – but also to show chivalry to the weak. When men and women meet as putative equals, they are all hit by conflicting drives. Men need to be sensitive to the balance between being courteously protective, being patronising and being taken for bullies. Equally, women must not let co-operative tactics be mistaken for weakness.

Some sense of competition is vital, but an overdose can leave women adrift. Often competition takes a low priority for them. For example, there can be few more adversarial and competitive jobs than being a barrister. Barristers spend time opposing one another by publicly supporting conflicting stories for a judge and jury to weigh up. Success as a barrister is counted by numbers of cases won. For one young female barrister, this is a misguided approach. 'You're taught not to get involved with clients. It's an unwritten code: you're just a lawyer, stand back. But lawyers use it as a cop-out. Surely what lawyers have is a greater responsibility for sorting people's problems out – not simply being adversarial at the bar. My day may be four hours with the client, and ten minutes in court – is that overstepping bounds? My male colleagues would think so. They'd say I was turning into a counsellor or a therapist. But I think it's important to distinguish the ultimate legal solution from the needs of the client. You have to get away from 'win or lose'. If you're doing a child abuse case – what's winning? I settle well over half my cases before they come to court. But I can't discuss this with my male colleagues, because I'm afraid of being categorised as emotional.' Where men identify a fight, and prepare the confrontational behaviour which goes with it, women may see a totally different dynamic in which the notion of 'winning' is completely irrelevant.

## Feelings

Men act, women feel: according to the stereotype, women are more emotional than men. It's not that men don't have emotions. Laboratory tests reveal that men show much greater physiological reactions to external stimuli than do women – but they don't talk about them, as women do. Women's technique of expressing what they feel can reduce damaging physical impact, but, if they take it to extremes, they can become depressed by their dependence on other people in handling their emotional responses. Men find it natural to disguise their feelings, but it costs them in wear and tear on their physical resources. More men commit suicide than women, and men take refuge in alcohol to a greater extent. However, most men no longer believe they can produce the results they need in an emotional vacuum, and become very irritated if it is suggested to them they don't talk about feelings and don't know how to handle them. It's a mark of the New Man that he can and does. But it remains hard even for the New Men to show feelings in the professional arena – because they need a modicum of intimacy to make expressing emotions feel natural and safe. Indeed, it may feel very unsafe to express some emotions, because they actually create intimacy – which, men feel, is distinctly out of place in working life. In private, they have learned, there are benefits in abandoning the mask, but professional encounters happen on a public stage where a front must be maintained. So, while they acknowledge it's OK to show emotion, the emotions it's OK for them to show are limited. It's rare for men in the course of their work to display any emotions beyond anger or a huge, boyish enthusiasm. If they do mention other feelings, they tend to be ones from the distant past. It's much more difficult to get them to say how they feel *now* – a thing women are much more used to doing. What's more, it may be OK for men to behave irritably, say, but it's much less common for them to admit that they feel irritable, or discuss what it means to others when that's how they feel.

I know men can display other emotions even in professional spheres because I have seen them do it – but usually only when invited, or when it's a special occasion, or have seen the example given by a woman, and usually when they are in a group of which women comprise at least half. One female manager made it a strict rule to keep home and work separate, even to the extent of not talking about any aspect of her home at work. She is extremely good at her job, but hard to get to know, because of this reticence – much like a man, in fact. One day during a workshop she decided to talk about how a domestic crisis prompted a work decision. It was a moving story, which had three beneficial results. She broke a barrier in giving away this secret in a work environment: it didn't harm her, she found, but gave her the pleasure of helping others to share her experience and test their own reality. Secondly, the mixed group who heard the story found it revealing about her as an individual, which made her more accessible to us all. Thirdly, the story inspired others to describe how personal matters had influenced their careers. The men found it very difficult to express their feelings – but they did it. One chap told his story in the third person, poker-faced: 'Once upon a time there was a young account executive who was very happily married but did not want children . . .' He said later there was no way he could have done it without that distancing effect. In that situation dropping barriers and revealing emotional reactions generated intimacy. Intimacy created bonding. Bonding increased loyalty, heightened motivation to work together effectively, deepened understanding. We used the information as clues for working together more productively, not as definitive and repressive judgments.

But workshops are different from real life. It's much more likely that exposing an area of vulnerability at work will be seen by some men as a measure of weakness to be exploited, rather than a strength which contributes to the professional relationship. Your secrets are *not* safe with me, in other words. Show me your soft underbelly – but I'll keep my own defences in place.

The restricted emotional spectrum created by men has come to seem the normal pattern for the workplace. If women show fewer inhibitions in demonstrating emotion they can appear vulnerable and out of step; many therefore suppress them in order to maintain the accepted masculine pattern. Recent research suggests that the incidence of alcoholism and stress-related heart disease is increasing among 'working women'.

It is sex-appropriate for women to display fear, hurt, guilt and trouble. But anger is less permissible, as it has been all their lives. When anger is what they feel, many women have difficulty in finding an 'acceptable' way of expressing it. This is partly because they haven't had the practice, and partly because shows of anger from women elicit disconcerted and disconcerting reactions from the people they deal with. It may turn inward and become depression, or explode when women have held on to frustration for so long that there is nothing else for it.

When men talk about women and their emotions, they usually mean tears. Alec Reed, Chairman of Reed Personnel, accepts this aspect: 'They're more emotional – you're prepared for a woman to break down in tears, but it shouldn't be a loss of face for her. You just walk out and let her compose herself.' Lovely. Pick up the agenda again when things are back to normal – i.e. when public demonstrations of feeling have quietened down. Of course there's value in allowing time for an emotional reaction – but it's also important that walking out is perceived as a supportive response, and not a tactic for opting out of exploring the causes. The emotional accompaniment many men say they fear most is tears. At counselling workshops where an actor – male or female – played a distressed employee, I've seen male managers ignore the phenomenon of tears, deflect them by being cross so as to reduce its impact on themselves, cope superbly by expressing support and understanding and sensitively awaiting the right moment to move into 'action' mode, or melt in a helpless puddle of heartache.

Some men regard tears as a cynical use of inappropriate behaviour. Others are just plain terrified, because they don't know how to respond. Others again are sceptical about men's real, underlying attitude to weeping females. One male manager said: 'I think all this talk about the acceptability of women crying is disingenuous. With a woman in tears at least you know where you are – in charge, in the position of protector. Most men would find well-aimed, justified, devastating anger from a woman much more terrifying. Tears are a welcome alternative.' Magnanimously accepting visible distress from women may be a way of battening down the hatches against displays of more unsettling emotion.

There are men whose work technique demands that they *make* females weep. I once witnessed the end of an incident in which a teacher in his late thirties was admonishing an eleven-year-old girl who'd failed (most heinously) to hand in her homework. She stood smiling while he became more and more irate. Finally she broke down, and he dismissed her. He saw me watching, and said defensively: 'I had to make her cry to be sure she'd got the message.' Her smile had convinced him she was not taking it on board. I'd say it was more likely she used it as a method of self-control. A deadpan face tips too easily into obvious distress, so she over-compensated to avoid it. He tried harder to break her – and won.

Such methods won't always work, though. A software marketing manager told how the first time she was called into the Managing Director's office he enumerated her mistakes without warning in a long tirade. 'He reduced me to a snivelling wreck. Six months later he summoned me again, and I marched straight in and told him I wasn't going to take another bollocking like the last one.' Men can be very frightening, but you can learn to cope – by going on the offensive.

Even if women do have permission to break down in public, there is still a residue of thinking that it's inappropriate to let less dramatic feelings leak into the professional agenda. In mixed groups the agenda is held by the men unless women make a mighty effort or a women is in charge. So, even if women are attentive to their own feelings and those of others they, too, hesitate to express them. The result can be meetings at which half the members are frustrated and annoyed, but nobody says so. A young executive at Reed Personnel maintains: 'The only reasonable thing to do is to accept the facts. Emotions cloud proper judgments, and should be suppressed. If you've made your decision based on facts you can give an answer. Sometimes the truth can hurt. It's necessary to make a difference to people's lives rather than be wishy-washy and bring emotions into it – because everyone sees them differently.' Even young men feel that decision and action can be undertaken independent of the feelings they arouse, whereas women are more likely to take account of feelings – perhaps because they watch out for and read physical clues which men discount. It may be this which contributes to the phenomenon of 'women's intuition', which can seem magical and suspect when set against masculine 'judgment', based on concrete facts alone. In one 1992 sexual discrimination case, part of a report on the female manager concerned was quoted, to show how she had fallen short of expectation: 'She seemed to come to conclusions by intuition rather than by facts, and there were many occasions of a lack of professionalism.' (She was eventually reinstated.) The masculine formula is 'Professional behaviour depends on things which are measurable and consistent.' Robots operate exclusively on things which are measurable and consistent. But humans aren't robots, and how they feel as individuals add up in the end to company morale.

Putting emotion on the agenda at work doesn't mean letting it guide the outcome to the exclusion of all else, but it can have a positive effect on individuals and therefore their job performance. During the recession of the early Nineties, many companies streamlined their operations by getting rid of people. Survivors did receive corporate messages intended to maintain morale, but only rarely an opportunity to air how they felt to decision-makers within the company. The leaders' line was that, however everyone felt about it, those redundancies had to happen, and it was futile to belly-ache about it. Listening to the pain wouldn't change a thing. We ran a series of workshops for one company in the aftermath of reorganisation. The delegates welcomed them as an opportunity to off-load all the suspicion, fear and stress they were suffering, preparatory to planning strategies for improving the situation. The process revealed – to themselves as much as to the leaders of their organisation – their underlying bedrock of loyalty and positive goodwill. Negative feelings don't disappear when unacknowledged. Confronting them can produce constructive results, whereas leaving them to fester can be damaging to the company. If employees feel bad about their company, what happens when the economy picks up and jobs are easier to get? They vote with their feet.

Permitting feelings to be a factor in working life is not an excuse to wallow in the irrelevant, but a way to achieve professional goals. The strength of the masculine approach to emotion is a sense of control – up to a point. The strength of the feminine approach to expression of feelings is its honesty – up to a point. People trapped in a sex-role stereotype can find their handling of emotion unsuccessful: keeping quiet about negative feelings can increase the damaging effects of stress; displaying them can invite attack or lead to dependency and depression. Long-term benefits can be gained if women and men can move away from the extremes of their own sex-role stereotypes, by observing the opposite sex and picking up tactics which produce the most constructive results. Women can facilitate the process of giving emotions the right level of import-ance, but this will only be valuable if they are used as a tool of strength, not an admission of weakness.

## Parallel universes

The kinds of challenge men and women face are similar. They have to get on with other people, make things happen, get what they want, persuade others to do things. Their responses to these challenges are different, because they have grown up with very different experiences under the influence of the expectations of the culture they grew up in. Men are consummate actors out on the public stage. They act with confidence, they deny weakness, they ensure something visible is always happening, and value is attrib-uted to all those things – so that anything different becomes less valuable. Women are less skilled at acting in this way, but may try, if it seems that their habitual methods won't get them anywhere. Women are more likely honestly to express self-doubt, to display their own feelings and allow for those of others, to adopt a non-confrontational style which encourages co-operative behaviour.

The perceptions of daily activity at work which men and women describe give an impression less of a shared world than of two parallel universes – similar enough to deceive their inhabitants into thinking they are portraying identical events, but actually so subtly different as to produce pitfall after pitfall when their inhabitants attempt to act together on the information they receive. Men and women may think they're saying the same things; they may think they're behaving perfectly normally and comprehensibly; but reac-tions and interactions often prove they've miscalculated. It's likely that women understand men's universe better then men understand women's – and that they are unhappier about it. Deborah Tannen, in her book *You Just Don't Understand*, describes a series of research exercises which compared how men talk when they're together, how women talk together, and what happens in mixed groups. When women and men get together, they discuss things of mutual interest, but in a way which is much closer to the way men talk together: a way which seems, to women, more superficial, more data-driven, less probing. Both sexes, says Tannen, make adjustments to their natural style when they are together, but women make more, and therefore tend to be less satisfied with the dealings they have. Women have to listen and observe whan men do, because the parameters, on the whole are set by men. They can choose to support a universe that doesn't suit them, or encourage greater understanding of their own.

In the working world men are the natives. They wear the uniform, they speak the language, they create the base-line, they set the rules, they define the culture. Natives have a way of doing things which habit has rendered sacred, and divergences from it take up a lot of time and space. It's unnatural trying to accommodate outsiders. But not doing so can increase the sense of exclusion which outsiders may start with. It may be that women are picking up more of a sense of exclusion than men believe they're giving. Many men would indignantly deny that they treat women as outsiders at all. They would claim, sincerely, that they regard women as having as much right to inclusion as they do. Many people, both men and women, would say that all this native and outsider set-up is total overkill. Any sense of exclusion is a delusion, and anyone who complains of it is paranoid. Certainly, sensitivities range enormously among members of both sexes, as does sophistication in dealing with the results. Often pain is minimal: there is only a temporary and jolting reminder that women cannot take their inclusion for granted. The awkwardness is not all on one side; everyone is trying to find a level on which they can operate. But all of us know we are working to different rules. And the fundamental perceptions – by men of women and by women of men – dictate how interactions between them subsequently operate.

Any woman with common sense is going to decide that peaceful co-existence with the natives demands first that she understands the prevailing language and culture. Joining in at first may be a bit halting and pidgin. The natives may have a variety of perceptions of the newcomers. Are they visitors? A temporary phenomenon, to be catered for (short-term only) until they go away? Are they tourists? Not really something to be taken seriously: people whose meaningful existence is somewhere else, and who only impinge on the real world by getting in the way, although they have their uses in helping the economy? Spies, sniffing out precious secrets in order to devalue their importance? Invaders, taking over territory that is not theirs?

A more constructive reception is probably the one where the natives treat the newcomers as worthwhile immigrants: significant people with a perfectly viable and effective background, who nevertheless choose to become absorbed into another world, with the intention of both getting and giving value. Newcomers welcomed in that way provide a rich source of new ideas. They don't have to stop being different; they don't have to match all the behaviour the natives are used to; they can acceptably bring something new to the party. However, this approach still assumes that one group has more right than the other to be there, and to influence what happens.

The most positive approach of all is to see both sexes as natives of their own culture, and to assume a comparable foreignness for each in the other one. In an overview of research into gender at work, Valerie Hammond, Director of Research at Ashridge Management College, quotes a Swedish Managing Director, Bjorn Sprangare, who worked on communication issues with senior men and women in his company: 'We became more and more aware of how differently women and men think and act. It is quite simply a question of two cultures meeting. It is like coming to a foreign country.'

We need to compile a sort of mental phrasebook of perceptions, to distinguish where the main, habitual differences lie. An understanding of where translations don't tally can enable each sex to make more sense of the other, across the gulf between parallel universes. Each sex can use their fresh understanding to interpret the other's behaviour more accurately, in order to identify mismatches, mistaken assumptions, and unquestioned prejudices. Once we know where and what they are, we can circumvent them and concentrate on performance. If we never acknowledge what the differences mean, they will continue to get in the way.

# 3 Interpreting the Other Half

The phrasebook needs to include some of the items which set off reactions when men and women meet at work: the immediate expectations they arouse, the images they present, the signals and symbols they use, the way they talk.

Given the facts, and the influences of habit and sex-role stereotype, women and men have contrasting expectations of one another at work – some reasonable, some less so. The scenery and accepted ways of working are mainly masculine. The facts about men at work are: it's mostly men who hold positions of power. There are more men in paid employment than women, overall. In most areas men were there first. Men at work have a longer history than 'working women'. Consequently, men tend to be tagged with a three-part expectation, every bit of it positive:

- Authority and power.
- Knowledge and competence.
- Normality and easy fit.

Expectations about 'working women' in areas where they are less common can come in four main parts:

- Service and care, because of the kinds of job a great many women do.
- Lack of knowledge, abnormality, unpredictability, helplessness: the reverse of what men represent.
- Unnaturalness: failure to be 'proper' women, because they're 'working' women.
- Sexuality, because they're women.

Part of the problem for 'working women' is that they are in a minority, especially at higher levels of an organisation. Members of significant minorities suffer more from being stereotyped, because (if we're charitable) nobody has quite enough experience of individuals to stop the stereotype taking over; or (if we're not) the stereotype itself is used as a way of preserving power. It protects members of the majority against experience, against having its ideas shaken up, against having to rethink.

Most 'working women' can do without parts two, three and four of the 'working woman' stereotype, and for some of us part one could be a bit suspect, too, if it means we're down to make the tea. Not everybody we meet will cram us into such negative pigeonholes, but some certainly will, and we can't know in advance who will, and which pigeonholes they will select.

## Image

If women as a sex generate impressions which are negative, or disconcerting, positively damaging, or at best grounds for caution, then those impressions tend to invalidate or undermine the messages women bring. Messages are never enough on their own. That's why Mrs Thatcher took elocution lessons and spent years redefining her image. Any salesperson knows that buyers buy not just the product but the promise – and the person making it. Too often the 'working woman' stereotype can get in the way of doing the job, so we have to find methods of combating it.

In my job, for instance, I am supposed to speak with authority and confidence. If I am to be effective, people must trust me sufficiently to act on what I say. I need to create a positive response which persuades people I am on their side and can deliver what I undertake. So I need to convince them I am warm, friendly, knowledgeable and authoritative. I can't do it by public announcement, as Elizabeth I is supposed to have done: 'I know I have the body of a weak and feeble woman, but I have the heart and stomach of a king – and of a King of England, too.' There's nothing I can do about my sex. Except on the telephone, where my light baritone leads me down many interesting byways with people who call me

'Sir', nobody can mistake me for anything other than a woman. I look like one, I dress like one, I giggle like one. However, I may need to modify some aspect of the impression I put across. This involves a series of choices, compensations and unnatural behaviour.

The first choice I make is what I call myself. My parents christened me Patricia Ann so that when I grew up I could be Patsy or Patsy-Ann or Trish or Trixie or Patty or Paddy. As it happens, I have always been known as Pat, undoubtedly because that is how I have always introduced myself. I've done this consciously, not because I'm rejecting my sex-role and pretending to be a man, but because nearly all the other options are fluffily ultra-feminine. Pat sounds stronger than Trish. How powerful would my message be if it emanated from a person called Trish? The use of 'masculine' abbreviations is a ploy which other women adopt. In 1991 Carol Johnson and Helen Petrie of the University of Sussex conducted research into what women call themselves. They found that a quarter of their sample of women chose to shorten their names to ones which could be of either sex. Men never shorten theirs to something that could be female. Some women certainly seem to feel that by calling themselves Jo or Sam or Sandy or Chris or Nick they are more instantly credible in a man's world than women called Juliet or Linda or Diana. For those of us who do it, it is probably just an attempt to annihilate one unnecessary barrier, given that there are a multitude of others less easy to demolish. We are trying to turn off at source a potential for dismissive behaviour which diminishes 'feminine' females, because we fear it will detract from our other qualities, more relevant and productive. If authority is masculine, we will not blatantly label ourselves as feminine. Yet the names of Anita Roddick (of The Body Shop), Margaret Thatcher (first woman Prime Minister), Kate Adie (television journalist), Betty Boothroyd (first woman Speaker of the House of Commons), evoke impressions of authority, not womanly weakness. If enough messages from people called Trish and Lindy-Lou and Petronella are taken seriously, maybe in the end the names will take on gravitas – or become irrelevant.

The next choice is title. No value judgments accompany Mr. Mr just means you're a man. Back in the Seventies, when the title Ms was invented, it meant 'Don't categorise me as married or unmarried.' I would have none of it. I found it ugly and unpronounceable. For 20 years as Miss Dixon I had felt like a flighty flibbertigibbet, and I couldn't wait to be Mrs Somebody – matronly, grown-up, labelled at last a success! Only when my divorce came through did I start, reluctantly, to call myself Ms: because Mrs wasn't true, and Miss seemed a little virginal, given the brace of toddlers clinging to my skirts.

The idea of Ms in the Seventies was that it would replace Mrs and Miss. It hasn't. It has just added a third category. The one you choose still tells people not only you're a woman, but what kind of woman you are. I gather from one group of women in their twenties that nowadays Miss means 'unwanted', and Mrs means 'written off'. It turns out, according to American research, that by adopting the title Ms you become judged as higher in competence, ability, leadership skills, ambition and success than anyone called Miss or Mrs. Ms does more than just disguise your marital status. It implies: 'I mean business, and it's completely irrelevant whether I'm married or not.' However – and here's the downside – the research also suggests that a Ms is much less warm, likeable and friendly than a Miss, Mrs or Mr. A Mr is still seen as the most masculine – but Ms runs it close. And from a man's point of view, Ms probably offers the greatest risk of being wrong-footed.

A survey of female American business executives under 40 showed that the majority chose the title Ms. In Britain there is more resistance to Ms than in the States. Many women say they would prefer not to use a title at all. But we have to. Miss Elizabeth Neville, Assistant Chief Constable of Sussex Police, says: 'My main aim is to avoid causing embarrassment for other people. Women have all the wrong options, and I dislike every one of them. But if I don't use a title in letters everyone assumes I'm a man, because most people in my rank are.' We have the flexibility of choice, certainly, but what we choose is likely to mark us out as either warmly feminine or professionally competent (but not both) – or simply male by default. If lots of us go on long enough using the title Ms, perhaps warmth will creep into it.

Next choice: what to wear. I get up in the morning and prepare myself for a world which is mostly peopled by men. My two male colleagues put on their suits, choose a tie, and they're off. Whatever they wear they are going to merge with the dominant crowd. Menswear for the white-collar workplace has developed as a uniform to eliminate differences. It has been known for men to compare their socks. If they match, it's worth a congratulatory word. Conformity means safety, brotherhood, belonging. (Well, that's how it looks to me. An alternative explanation is this, offered by a man: 'Maybe it's not togetherness, so much as a grateful sense that here is one area where competition is off the agenda – for today, at least . . .') As soon as men put their clothes on they become camouflaged as one of the chaps: so much so that, as one woman pointed out: 'A prat can look a genius by wearing a suit.' There's no way I can look anything but different.

In any case, my objective is not the same. I have to look as good as I can. If I don't look good, then I have a major problem, because I am then not credible as a woman. Women don't judge men primarily on looks, so although men care greatly how they appear, a physical fault or a spot on the nose won't usually have them rocked to their foundations and questioning their personal identity. Not for them all the boring things women do as a matter of course to compensate for their shortcomings, real or perceived: blusher and hairdo to make a thin face wider, boxy jackets to disguise the derrière, overnight cream to keep wrinkles at bay. My credibility is weighed in the balance before I have ever opened my mouth, because women are judged on how they appear. The gorgeosity factor stalks offices and factories as well as magazines and parties.

Lisa Armstrong, while fashion editor of the *Independent*, said: 'We're prisoners of our looks. There's so much less for a man to go wrong.' What we look like matters, whatever our function. When Preisler and Buggins – two highly paid City women – were slugging it out in the courts over an important case concerning maternity pay and constructive dismissal, they were described as follows (by a woman) in the *Evening Standard* of 19 December 1991: 'Preisler, the more physically appealing of the two . . . Buggins, thinner, more elegant and hard faced . . .' The competition may have started on the basis of principle, but it managed to develop into a beauty contest. It's often a surprise to find which women are sensitive to the issue of looks. Profiled in the *Sunday Times* in

January 1992, before she became Deputy Leader of the Labour Party, Margaret Beckett was quoted as saying: 'Nobody has ever accused me of being beautiful, and I certainly didn't welcome the televising of the Commons, because the camera loves beautiful people. I'd have liked obscurity until the next generation, but there you are. People would rather look at a pretty young face and I don't blame them – so would I, but it doesn't help me.'

So one criterion for how to dress is to make yourself fit to take part in the parade of female youth and beauty. If you don't, there's something wrong with you. If you do, then you're back to clashing with the stereotype: authority is masculine, you look like a woman, so you don't carry authority with you and you may have to fight to be perceived as a serious contender at work. Not only that, but men's image means work, whereas women's image has sexual connotations. This brings a new range of criteria to take into account, if you want to make yourself acceptable in the workplace, and display the image that will most effectively assist you to do your job.

The safest way to dress for white-collar work is a boringly bland, orthodox modification of male dress, with a discreet length of leg peeping out below. This is the classic suit recommended in the magazines for 'working women'. It's probably grey or blue, with delicate touches of white at the neck and cuffs. Compromises are becoming more common, and moving the working wardrobe nearer to a non-working wardrobe: brighter colours, shorter skirts, more stylish shapes. However, on the whole, convention rules. If you're trying to create an air of authority there has to be a jacket. It performs two vital functions: it confers class, for one, by affirming executive status. Joanna James, a venture capitalist, reckons she gets instant hierarchical credibility by this simple means: 'Chaps automatically think: "If a woman is wearing a jacket she can't be a secretary, and if she's in she must be good, because she's in."' The second function of the jacket is to wipe out all evidence of bosoms. A male senior manager is quite positive about the consequences when this does not happen. 'Breasts defeat the point of meetings. If I have to deal with a business associate with breasts, I feel conned – by her and her company. She gets my attention but not my business.' Similarly, trousers won't do. 'Oh, no. Trousers mean you can see the line of the buttocks.' This man has to shut out sex to make business happen. While there's an element of sense in this, it's a tortuous chain of logic and a ludicrous apportionment of responsibility. If female secondary sexual characteristics are not firmly denied, but visible, then they must be on blatant display; therefore their proprietor is to blame for tempting him to deviate from his agenda – which must mean she is not serious about business.

The perception of men like this is not women's doing – but they have to cope with the consequences. A forty-year-old retailer threw the question back at women: 'OK, I can accept that men don't know how to interpret sexuality which isn't theirs; but do women know how to display independent feminism rather than female sexuality? If a woman at work wears fishnet stockings or her cleavage is visible, what is she saying? Is she saying: Look how desirable I am? Or: I am what I am, and I wear what I like, and you can accept it or not?' This could be construed as women's problem of image or men's problem of interpretation. Both men and women need to cultivate common sense and eschew naïveté.

Anthea Yamey is an image consultant who deals with both men and women. She says: 'Image matters. It's not fair – but it's a fact. There are women in places where they would never have been thought of 25 years ago, and there are rules to abide by. You can say the rules are there to solve men's problems – and you'd be right. What you have to do is learn the rules, then break them if you choose – but face the consequences. Understand that there will be a reaction. You are in control. Don't close doors before you get to them. Get in first, then close the doors behind you if you choose.' The rules boil down to minimising every potential source of sexual temptation. This cuts out a lot of extreme ways of dressing, including fishnet tights, leather mini-skirts, low-cut blouses, tousled tresses. Fair enough, since you're there to do a job, not catch a man. But sometimes there seems to be a fine line between preventing enticement and preserving identity.

I heard a story about a judge, an elderly man, before whom appeared a young female barrister. The barrister began to speak. The judge cupped a hand to his ear. 'I can't hear you,' he said. She started again, a little louder. 'I still can't hear you,' said the judge. Somewhat flustered, because she had not met this problem before, she made a third attempt. 'I tell you what,' said the judge, 'I might be able to hear you better if you remove those earrings.' The barrister swallowed hard, and removed them. 'That's fine,' said the judge. 'No problem now.' Across a generation and a gender gap, Establishment Man in his sixteenth-century wig had scored a point and scarred a barrister – and influenced the barrister's client, who had thus seen the custodian of his defence reduced to an apparently unprofessional frippet. Earrings are not exactly a secondary sexual characteristic. That judge's message seemed to be that *any* sign which reflected that barrister's gender was inappropriate. For some men, women are not welcome in the workplace, and the way to let them know it is to attack any overt signs of their gender in order to diminish them professionally.

There are unassailable reasons for women to make it clear they are not sex objects – but do they have to go so far as to deny they are women? Women tried that, back in the Eighties, when they wore pseudo-male suits and ties. Anthea thinks the power dressing craze was a military response: women drawing up the battle lines with an opposing and complementary standard of their own. The fiercest heat of the battle is over. What's left is an uneasy truce, and so the uniform can afford to be softened. Anthea is optimistic that women need not emulate men any more. What they need to do, she thinks, is to present a safe, conventional image, as men do, leaving flamboyance and eccentricity for the powerful few or those who don't give a damn. That way everyone we deal with is secure without knowing why, and we never look as though we've put in an inappropriate degree of effort. However, you can't win them all: some men think women take staid conformity too far. Sir Nicholas Fairbairn, MP for Perth and Kinross, gave an interview to the *Spectator* in July 1992. He was incensed because female MPs *don't* emphasise their femininity. 'They lack fragrance, on the whole . . . Maybe in this day and age with all these hang-ups, they deny their femininity . . . Why has womankind given up the exaltation of herself – that attempt to attract, to adorn, to glint? They all look as though they are from the 5th Kiev Stalinist machine-gun parade.' The *Daily Telegraph* reported mixed reactions from female MPs, ranging from outrage to amusement.

Every item we wear is a word, Anthea says, and they combine to make a sentence which sums us up. The question is: what is that sentence? I met a Marketing Director who had made one interpretation and was keen to test it out. He was wearing a pale grey suit, a white shirt, a tactful tie and chestnut brogues. I was wearing a fuchsia jacket, black shirt and skirt. 'Tell me,' he said, à propos of my outfit, 'When women wear all the gear, with the shoulder-pads and all that, are you saying: "Fuck you!"?' Certainly not: such a reading had never occurred to me. But other men may be wondering the same thing, failing to ask the question, and acting on the assumption that it's true.

There are risks, however women dress. Women wear clothes in a certain way to express how they feel about themselves. Having to compensate for other people's misperceptions reduces women's freedom to modify conventional garb in even a subtle way; and this can feel like having to blank out some of what makes you who you are. Elizabeth Neville: 'I want to please myself – but also not give completely the wrong message, and it's so hard to judge what you're putting across. Uniform helps a lot. The only room for speculation then is whether it's tights or a suspender-belt you're wearing – and there's plenty of that.' Anthea Yamey is confident that it's to everyone's advantage – not least to the organisation – that people are happy with the way they look. Feeling good means performing better. Men take more persuading than women that their image matters, but it's scepticism rather than resistance. They generally start from a more complacent basis as it is. Men don't, on the whole, tot up their faults as sticks to beat themselves with, because they expect to look rather than be looked at. For women to feel good *and* avoid unnecessary trouble in the workplace can sometimes be a tall order.

Women do need to establish their own identity, particularly in areas where the extent of their contribution is threatened, and one way to do it is to make it acceptable to look different. Serious articles in *The Times* in November 1992, about the conceptual issues aroused by the General Synod's vote to allow women to enter the priesthood, were accompanied by a full colour photograph of a model in an embroidered chasuble with a frilly dog-collar. At about the time of a survey into the Bar which concluded that discrimination against women was rife, articles appeared demonstrating that women barristers ought to be permitted to wear something which was not a mere imitation of masculine uniform.

It is not a trivial matter. However, there is far too much psychological baggage about. Whereas women readily accept other women's image – because they have faced the same choices themselves, and know the issue is not about sex or fashion-plates, but identity – men are often too easily distracted into interpreting messages from women which they are not, in fact, giving. Professional competence and authority are discounted under irrelevant perceptions connected with gender, as though femaleness and competence could not co-exist. Of course not all reactions from men are as extreme, as defensive or as hostile as those I've recounted, but they happen.

More baggage: men's perception of themselves as the embodiment of normality at work. This leads them to misinterpret the difficulties women face. Men don't have to think twice about their image for work, because their names, their titles, their suits are the default, and they have far fewer options. Two of my colleagues are called John. A sturdy, ancient name – heart-of-oak and stalwart, and top of the list of names which imply (simultaneously and sight unseen) warmth, virility and authority. If they thought about it at all, they would regard such a reputation as only their due. But they don't think about it, because it isn't a problem. They point out – and I wholeheartedly agree – that personality, experience, preferred approach and skill all contribute to the success of our professional tasks. They think I overestimate the effect of gender; I think they make too little of it. They are instantly acceptable, and can get straight to what they have to do. Of course, they then have to work hard to deliver – but it seems to me that my female colleagues and I have to work hard for acceptability before we get the all-clear to start delivering. Being a man gives you authority until you prove you don't deserve it; being in the brotherhood absolves you of emitting sexual signals, consciously or otherwise. There is nothing to defend yourself against or compensate for, except the challenges inherent in the job itself.

Women's baggage is over-anxious sensitivity to the reactions they encounter as they try simultaneously to get it right for work and maintain identity and self-esteem. It is necessary to be realistic, and if that means saving extreme expressions of identity for the weekend, then so be it. As far as the workplace is concerned, it is more important to be accepted as a fully-fledged occupant than to be deflected into spending precious time worrying about externals. Embroidered chasubles will have their place in due course, but for now the primary goal is to accept that there will always be misreadings, and the sane course is to sigh deeply and move on.

## Signals and symbols

Mismatches of perception don't stop with image: they continue into personal transactions. The handshake is the first point of contact. Books on the successful use of body language tell you that touch – as a decider in a selling situation, for instance – carries a knock-out message. One book contains a neat matrix showing how length of shake, warmth and moistness of hand, and strength of grip interrelate to give a certain impression; people undertake a complicated swop of signals in the few seconds it takes to shake hands. Nobody loves a wet fish, of either sex. High-tension power handshakes make many people feel insecure. Of all the permutations given in the research results, there is not even one which awards a completely positive rating to a woman. The best kinds of handshake given by a man define him as confident, warm, co-operative, empathic and successful; the same quality of handshake from a woman labels her as unfeminine, threatening and aggressive. If you shake firmly, you're potentially aloof, cold and hostile; if your handshake is short, you can come across as incompetent. There's another problem, too: that of separating professional signals from personal signals. There's always the fear that if you make your handshake too warm, you may look as though you're giving a come-on. Come on, chaps, what chance have women got?

Many of the observable differences between men and women make it easier for men to be dominant in situations where both sexes are present. Most men are taller and bigger than most women. Many women are faintly conscious that they are at a physical disadvantage. At points of disagreement in a debate, they are aware of a residual nervousness which has nothing to do with the matter on the agenda. They don't really expect the men they work with to become violent and overpower them – but they could. So they may back off. Psychologist Jane Firbank was quoted in the *Guardian* of 5 May 1992 on the subject of negotiation. 'Negotiation for men is the stuff of life, sport brought into the boardroom. For women it is not a game. They are not so competitive, and for them negotiating with men strikes basic fears. It can feel threatening to deal with a man when you have a vague awareness that he is bigger than you. In the context of a boardroom deal, that may sound ridiculous, but it is there underneath.'

It's easier to get attention if you are large, loud, unselfconscious and 'normal'. How do you compensate for being small, slight and soprano? One response is to overdo it: stand tall, dress powerful, shout loud. Women who adopt such methods are perceived very negatively indeed. It's also hard to do, because it's anti-cultural and we haven't been trained for it. Some would answer that it's not necessary – but the evidence is that size is always correlated with status and authority. Shorter people have to look up to taller people. In one study it was found that management employees – i.e. people in high-status occupations – are taller than non-management, regardless of gender. A woman professor reported that male students frequently touched and stroked her, because she was small and slight – which they wouldn't have done with a six-foot man. In studies of adolescent boys, the ones who lag behind in the puberty stakes are less likely to be taken into account in any group, let alone be able to lead it. Deeper voices, greater height, give a base-line of authority.

But it's not an insuperable handicap unless you think it is. I've worked with a woman of five foot whose height never comes into it until you are surprised to find, as you try to stand shoulder to shoulder, that she's standing shoulder to waist. Her presence is so big that it disguises her body size. On the other hand, I know a six-foot white Englishwoman whose height is usually the first thing on men's agendas, often to her detriment (because it makes her a Big Woman, which is abnormal); and a six-foot black American woman whose height, she says, is a benefit. The difference may simply be a matter of personality and positive thinking. Or it may be (counter-intuitively, perhaps) that the American's obvious foreignness makes life easier for her than for a British six-foot woman. She's foreign in a respectable way. A statuesque black American in Britain brings a whole different set of assumptions which grant permissions that a large English rose may not be allowed.

Something like 70 per cent of any message put across comes from body language. In their book *Sex and Gender*, John Archer and Barbara Lloyd quote research which makes it clear that gestures which demonstrate dominance are the ones which men use, while women use more submissive body language. Men stare: women lower their eyes and look away. If two men work together, it is the one with the higher status who initiates touch (slap on the back, arm round shoulder): among men and women, it is men who do the touching. Men crowd space: women yield it and move away. Men frown and look stern: women smile. Archer and Lloyd suggest that the connection between dominance gestures and gender comes as a surprise to many people, who believe they are simply obeying convention or being polite, not physically demonstrating inequality. Trying to compensate for this imbalance, however, can be counter-productive if its objective is misunderstood. If women use body language in the way that is natural to them they risk being seen – and treated – as submissive; if they echo what men do, they risk being perceived as aggressive and unfeminine. Men who behave dominantly are seen as more masculine; women who behave dominantly are seen as less feminine. Back to the old either/or. Behaving naturally for a woman doesn't get you the attention you need; behaving unnaturally for a woman can, but it's hard to do, may be misunderstood or perceived negatively, and may undermine identity. Take gaze, for instance. Many women find it hard to hold gaze, and to stay cool when being looked at. Habit and lack of confidence get in the way. When all heads are swivelling towards me, I wonder why. I stutter and stall. Is there a smut on my nose? Have I behaved unbecomingly? Have I said something foolish? Last of all comes the cheerful thought that I may be saying something worth hearing. Averting gaze is more comfortable, but builds up men's sense that they are in charge, which may not be the best route to fulfilling the job. If a woman holds a gaze with a man, the implication is not cool equality but hostility or sexual interest.

Thinking about the effect of 'natural' behaviour, and trying to compensate for its weaknesses, are enough to make anyone self-conscious about interactions with the opposite sex. There are plenty of occasions on which the difference between women and men is indicated by symbol or convention. Each on its own may be of minor significance, but the effect accumulates. For instance, there's the way men deal with issues of good manners: another pointer to their attitude towards women's status in the workplace. Once I walked down a street with an accountant who harangued me at length about the iniquities of giving women equal pay, because, he maintained, it's ridiculous to suggest women and men are equally valuable. As we came to various crossings and turned left and right, he waltzed madly behind me from side to side of the pavement. The aim was to keep on my outside, so as to protect me in a thoroughly nineteenth-century manner from the splashing of imaginary carriages as they passed. He said, as he continued to maintain that women are inferior specimens in the workplace, that he hoped I didn't mind him doing this, as it was the right thing to do for women. Ostensible good manners can be a way of putting outsiders in their place.

Which is why a lot of men aren't sure whether to open doors for women or not. They have been caught before by women interpreting courtesy as put-down. (And sometimes those women were right). Men have a simple code of etiquette for women, and another one for men. Men take turns to open doors for one another, or the 'host' does the honours. If a man opens a door for a woman, she may find his behaviour offensive because it draws attention to her gender, where she thinks gender should be irrelevant; if he doesn't, she may regard him as not much of a man. It's not simple any more; conscious decisions have to be made, instead of going by the old rule-book. Women need to take an active role and do it their way, rather than waiting to fit smoothly into courtesies which may be out of place. But they should give men the benefit of any doubt about motive.

One way of ensuring the integration of women is the use of politically correct, non-exclusive vocabulary. Yes, we all know that the masculine subsumes the feminine and the plural the singular, as the lawyers put it. But it's no longer enough to fall back on that. One manager gave a presentation on company values to his staff. It contained a slide with the caption: 'Men or boys?' By this simple device, he excluded 15 per cent of his workforce from admission to the values. (And it was the men in the audience who pointed this out to him afterwards.) Trying to change this can feel very unnatural. In the company I work for there's a preponderance of women. We don't talk about 'man-power planning'. We have tried 'human-power' and 'people-power' and 'person-power' and they all make us feel we are making a point where there shouldn't be one. There simply isn't a natural-sounding terminology we can use. But tiny signs matter, and we persist. (In fact, the women were slower to adapt than the men). The same problem crops up when you are writing Terms and Conditions of employment, or job descriptions. You can apologise in advance for saying 'he', and make it simple but exclusive; or you can put 'he or she' or 's/he', and then decide whether to remain purist, by continuing with 'his or her', or ungrammatical by using 'their'. 'The Production Manager should appraise every member of their staff every six months . . .' Clumsy, in some ways, but preferable, and the shape of things to come. What starts off sounding artificial and robotic will end by tripping off the tongue neatly – and changing perceptions.

Tiny signs matter, but can seize disproportionate attention. Take beverages, for instance. Men drink pints, women pour tea. When I order my habitual pint of lager before dinner, I'm not making a statement: I'm very thirsty after a day running a workshop, and lager is what I drink. Most men can't resist a comment of some sort: 'Ah, very butch.' I've lost count of the times I've met raised eyebrows, or been advised to have it in two half-pint glasses. Some men are delighted, and some are embarrassed, or think there's been a mistake. An exceptional few take it in their stride.

As for tea, rare is the article about women's place in management which doesn't somehow get in a mention about the rejection, or cheerful acceptance, of a woman's part in the organisational tea ceremony. Rosemary Thorne, Sainsbury's first female Finance Director, was profiled in the *Daily Telegraph* in March 1992. 'She was pouring tea in her vast, pink office at Grand Metropolitan . . . She always pours tea at meetings, she says. The task just falls to her, because she is a woman. "It becomes a joke. I have never felt sensitive about things like that."' And yet serious advice often proffered to women who want to resist the 'service' aspect of the stereotype is: 'Never learn to type, never pour the tea.' Refreshment time can produce little moments where, whatever else is going on, the status of women as outsiders becomes boringly symbolised.

Because of the background of misinterpretation and attempts at compensation, men sometimes put women through a species of initiation ordeal, aimed to establish the state of integration they have reached. Early on, the man or group of men you have just met will do a few tests. They may use four-letter words or lavatory humour or tell risqué stories – with an apology up their sleeve just in case, and a weather eye open to see how you react. At twenty-one I'd been in my first teaching job for a week when the Religious Studies master (twice my age) told a convoluted story about marketing a sanitary towel, to me and two male colleagues (also twice my age). The punchline was: 'Not the best thing, but next to it!' They all looked at me. I was amazed. The story had come out of the blue. What was it for? I laughed. I never heard him do anything like it again. When such tests are undertaken, the idea seems to be to weigh up how much thought men need to give to modifying their behaviour. What kind of person is this? Does she understand the way we do things here? Can she take it? Can she be trusted to follow the pathways without making unnecessary waves? Can we let her be an honorary member of our club, or is she someone to keep out and treat according to different rules? Will she be intense and embarrass us, or hostile and reject what we say? Can we relax? Do we have to be on our guard – and if so, against what?

Men may harbour often misplaced suspicion about 'feminine wiles'. For men the term 'feminine wiles' seems to represent a mischievous variation on acceptable working vocabulary. Feminine wiles are Unfair Things Men Don't Do, to which the only possible response is to acknowledge gender rather than the job. They include tears, short skirts, coquettish activity, subtle flirtation, eyelash fluttering, and giggling. For some women these things are simply an intensive expression of La Différence. A male middle manager's view was this: 'Women should not have to prove themselves. They do not have to depend on feminine wiles. They can do as good a job as a man, but should neither have to behave like men in order to compete, nor expect 'special' treatment just because they are women.' The view of a female colleague of the same rank: 'It can pay to behave like a woman. We should not be afraid to achieve our objective by the use of feminine wiles if necessary. We should play to our strengths.' A more senior male manager: 'She's great – she doesn't use any feminine wiles at all – but I'm under no illusions as to what sex she is.' A parallel senior woman manager: 'Let's wheedle and whine, for Heaven's sake. It works!' A female Detective-Constable: 'I hate it when women flirt and giggle. Their behaviour tars me with the same brush.' Feminine wiles are not a myth, and some women do use them to excess, although probably not to anything like the extent men read into them. Taken to extremes they would be a kind of prostitution: using feminine behaviour to sell something or win someone over; the calculated use of sexual currency and gambits for the achievement of non-sexual aims. Not fair, not comfortable, not sensible. But men sometimes misinterpret feminine behaviour as sexual behaviour. While the workplace definitely does not require sexual behaviour, it does have a place for behaviour specific to women, if it is effective in achieving results.

As awareness creeps in that gender differences need to be taken into account, strategies for coping with them can make men and women self-conscious and distract the mind from the purpose of the job. What would it be like not to be self-conscious? Not to keep treading the circular path, or stumbling over the same old trip-wires? Men battle with the difficulties of interpreting the signals they receive, remembering where not to look, testing out where women stand, coping with surprise responses. As for women, they can't do what men do, because they are women, yet they can't rely on having the influence they need for the job if they behave as women do. Women find they are sending some signals uncon-sciously; and also consciously sending signals, consciously not sending signals, separating professional signals from personal sig-nals, not transgressing unspoken codes, trying to respond sensibly to the body language they read, and sitting in such a way that no one can see up their skirt. Talk about unspontaneous.

## Communication

**Airtime and Piracy.** Talking is powerful, and so is listening. But holding the floor and laying down the law, or interrupting a speaker, can look far more impressive to an audience than silent, thoughtful, head-nodding attention. Look at what happens in the seat of power. In the House of Commons we have a house divided into at least two separate factions, facing one another. Television cameras emphasise the visual nature of the encounters. The same rules apply as in small boys' school playgrounds: people are expected to be raucous, unsubtle and often rude. Point-scoring and adversarialism bring you notice and measure your effectiveness and your dominance. Listening isn't newsworthy. Making a noise is.

In any business set-up where men and women are present, it tends to be men who do the talking, and women the listening. Men get anxious if other men *don't* talk. Silence from men can be an exercise of power. Who is this guy? Does he know something I should? But they tend to expect women to keep quiet, so that women who have something they want to say need to make violent efforts to be heard. Eve Pollard, editor of the *Sunday Express*, was quoted in the *Financial Times* of 14 August 1992 as saying: 'You know how awful men are . . . I have to assert myself and say this amplified seventeen times, or they don't listen.' Talking is a way to take up territory and time. Listening feels so passive that it's very hard for men not to fill in the spaces. At workshops for men and women, the first and loudest contributors tend to be men. Women will eventually contribute willingly – but often only when courted. The opportunity to speak in a mixed group is rare enough to seem threatening to some women. A husband and wife team attended one workshop. Each time I invited the wife to speak, she deferred to him. Finally she erupted. 'Why are you picking on me?' she asked me. However, having once broken the ice she began to enjoy giving her own view of retailing, and ended up doing a song and dance act in front of the rest of the group.

As a rule, I talk less in meetings with clients than my male colleagues do. I don't break in, because it makes me feel as though I am being rude. My colleagues do interrupt. They feel a little indignant on behalf of their sex when I say how difficult I find it to get into the flow unless somebody makes an opening for me. They claim nobody's stopping women saying whatever they want to say. This is only true if women are prepared to behave like men: not to wait for an invitation, but to dive in regardless. Women who don't interrupt are polite but not powerful; women who do interrupt are powerful but not very nice. One youngish manager gets very irritated with the woman on his team. He says: 'She interrupts and stops the flow. She asks questions all the time. We're all doing fine, and she gets in the way. She's completely out of line.' He thinks she is being cheeky, and doesn't know her place; she can't find any other acceptable way of being included. At worst, she dissolves into tears, and he marks her record with comments about insubordination.

My colleagues and I facilitate workshops. Effectively this means orchestrating people's discussions and debate over time so that they supply the content of the meetings, whatever it is, and we guide it, summarise it, tie a neat bow around it, and hand it back. But some men often expect the 'leader' of a workshop to speak from power and authority – hand things down, not bring them out. At first they feel disappointed if they are encouraged to do the talking: they feel generating discussion is a sign of incompetence. And yet getting people to say what they really think only requires a certain skill, but airs more views, has more chance of reaching consensus, and lets everyone have a taste of ownership.

The power of communication ought to be redefined as 'saying the right thing at the right time', not 'saying something all the time'. Any man who lays claim to high-level communication skills normally means he can talk articulately and give a compelling presentation. He should be challenged to prove he can facilitate the other side of a conversation as well as delivering his own. Women must make their own space if it is not presented to them, and brave any negative response they encounter.

**Action or Acknowledgment.** One misinterpretation men often make about women is that they want their problems solved. Here's an example, told by a female Deacon in the Church of England. She is not entitled to lead the service of Holy Communion, but can assist by taking part in the distribution of the bread and wine. From time to time a person kneeling at the altar makes it clear, by word or action: 'Not from you. I can't take the Sacrament from a woman.'

While she understands why it comes about, this rejection hurts. Afterwards, she informs her male colleagues what has happened. She has come to expect two main reactions from them, and she recognises with gratitude that both are intended as support. One is muscularly Christian: 'Who was it? Come on, tell us, and we'll go and duff them up.' The men's response is to go into immediate action, and she finds it particularly heart-warming for its expression of solidarity. 'It's as though they were saying: 'Let's protect Our Woman,' she says. The second response is cooler. 'Well, I can tell you how that happens.' There follows a lengthy discussion about history and psychology, intended to solve her problem by giving her a context and an explanation. This response she finds unnecessary and faintly irritating. It fails to acknowledge the crux of her difficulty, which is that she has been rejected because of a factor which is unchangeable and integral to her existence. It assumes that intellectual understanding is enough to quieten pain.

The third kind of response is rare, and goes to the heart of her need, neither for action nor for solution, but for affirmation as a woman. She described one particular, treasured occasion, when the then Bishop of Bath and Wells, George Carey (now Archbishop of Canterbury), was present. He asked: 'How do you feel about that?' and listened to her answer. He acknowledged her account, and thanked her for making her quandary so plain. This was all she needed. The self-respect she had lost was reaffirmed.

Women can solve their own problems. They just like to create links by involving others in the process. They are saying 'This is how it is' not 'Tell me what to do' or 'Fix this for me'. Admitting trouble does not mean they are absolving themselves of responsibility for dealing with it, or that they are feeble. But often, that's how it's perceived – and many women learn to simulate the stiff upper lip and abandon the hope of sympathy, rather than risk being treated like a man, who would be giving a call to action if he told a story in which something had gone wrong. If women feel an impulse to tell a man about an experience, they may need to make it very clear that all they want is an audience to help them air their problem aloud. Men need to hold back from too swift a judgment, and from launching prematurely and uninvited into action mode.

**Bullshit vs Drivel.** Get women to describe the way men talk, and they'll often say men talk bullshit. 'It's futile,' said a female store manager about a colleague doing a similar job. 'All he does is take up time with words that lead nowhere.' It's an easy trait to caricature. If in doubt, make a noise, and don't worry overmuch about what it contains. Go for impact, speak from strength of personality, skate round doubt; sidestep probing challenge; gloss over missing logic or facts, attack, and put the other person on the defensive.

A senior manager in one company claimed, rather indignantly, when I asked him what he thought about women at work: 'Women talk drivel. I sat on a train and listened to a woman talking on her mobile phone. She went on and on about the little off-the-shoulder number she was going to wear that evening. What would you think if I went on about my little off-the-shoulder number?' Even women agree that women can sometimes make a meal out of trivia. A female Detective-Constable protested about some of her colleagues: 'Women make it easy for men not to value their input, by what comes out of their mouths. They're just silly and personal.' Sometimes they are, but sometimes it is a misperception: trivia are used as hooks on which to hang less superficial areas of experience. Women talk about how they feel, even when they are comparative strangers, and quite early in the process. I've had ten-minute conversations with strange women on the telephone, and felt I've understood them better than men I've dealt with for years.

Women's drivel makes men as impatient as men's bullshit does women. But while bullshit is forgivable, drivel is not. Although both sexes gossip, the term 'gossip' is negative and only belongs to the female stereotype. Women often feel – with some resentment – that bullshit is one of the optimum ways to get on in business. It is accepted as normal. Men need to be a little more selective in their judgments about what women say, and consider whether they are being complacent about the value and normality of what men say.

Women should use 'drivel' if it works, and it probably won't with men.

**Losing face, losing control.** Women talk about disasters, mistakes, weaknesses. For a man, admitting a weakness involves relinquishing control, losing face, slipping down the hierarchy. For a woman, it's a way of sharing common experience and getting comfort and sympathy. Men ask for help less than women do; asking for help means, for men, lending superiority to the giver, and, for women, making a connection to someone else.

A male colleague and I went to a meeting, at which we discussed a particular business issue which was creating a problem for our client. It was by no means clear to either of us what was the best thing to do, and we agreed that a good deal of thought would be required before we could come up with a solution. Afterwards, a female colleague asked us what we planned to do. I said: 'Oh, I don't know, it's all desperately confusing; I haven't a clue how to play it.' My thoughts were chaotic, and I didn't mind who knew it, so long as the client didn't. John was just as puzzled as I was; but what he said was: 'I haven't made a decision yet.' We had come to the same conclusion, but we chose different ways of expressing it. I wanted sympathy, and support in confronting the problem. The virtue in my approach was that I'd absorbed a bad reality and opened it up. The downside was that I sounded – even to myself – weak and helpless. The virtue in John's approach was that he sounded reassuring, masterful and in control. The downside (he says) was that he'd chosen a premature 'winning' stance rather than face squarely up to the challenge. Both approaches might be effective on the right occasion; but the expressions we chose to use would be likely, in a man's world, to mark John as a winner and me as an incompetent.

**Bridging the gaps.** Everybody will have their own repertoire of misunderstandings with the opposite sex, but there are some common themes. When men and women communicate, they can have the best of intentions, and still be talking at cross-purposes, and failing to fulfil one another's needs. Women have effective ways of making things happen: by keeping quiet, listening, getting others to talk, admitting their weaknesses, sharing doubt, soliciting understanding rather than solution. Whereas men see obvious value in what men do, because it's positive and active, many of them can't see what women are doing at all, and assume they're doing nothing. Women may be making a valuable contribution, but, if it's not recognised as such by men, feel forced to adopt a style of communication more common to men. This goes against the grain for women, and can be equally badly misunderstood by men.

If men begin to see that 'female' ways of communicating can also be interesting and effective, there can be big rewards. A man I have known for over twenty years went on a week's awareness course. The day he came back I noticed three things within the first half-hour, during which I did all the talking. One: I did all the talking. Two: he gave me dozens of silent permissions and encouragements to carry on talking: the head-nods, the eyes on my face, the complete absorption in my message. Three: when I stopped, he didn't leap in with an authoritative conclusion, closing the matter off for good and all ('Thank you, and goodnight'), but invited me to elaborate on what I'd said. When he became irritated at any of my comments, he said so, instead of just reacting to it, and we were able to move away from the disagreement more quickly. It was just as though he'd gone away and learned a language foreign to him, come back, and found it was one I'd been talking all that time.

The advantage to him in leaving space is that he can expect a complete response from me, instead of one curtailed by limitations he himself has set. For me, it's more like talking to a woman, with the exciting extra element of his male perspective. At work with his team he uses the skills he learned. He doesn't expect just to 'tell' someone something; he invites a response and allows time for it. This, he finds, helps to build relationships and uncover many problems at an embryonic stage, where they can be tackled before they create alarm and despondency throughout the business.

Awareness may indeed be the key, and it comes in three stages. Firstly, awareness of why we adopt the styles we do. Secondly, awareness that both styles of communication are effective and that there is nothing to stop both men and women operating both ways, given enough encouragement. Thirdly, awareness of the techniques required to make them both happen. Men need to take an active but silent part in the conversation, peppering their listening with the signals which mean: 'Go on, I'm listening, it's fascinating, say some more'. Women should cut down on some aspects of politeness: nodding in encouragement is a pleasant and motivating way to behave, but it extends monologues. If women want to be more influential they need to take active steps to procure more airtime.

Women at work are strangers in a strange land, where their effectiveness depends on their level of integration – which is created by a combination of their efforts and those of men. Men and women misunderstand each other all the time. How we look, and how we say what we say, lead to a Babel of incomprehension which is all the worse because we generally don't discuss it, or check that we are talking the same language. As was said of America and England: two nations divided by a common tongue.

The road to comprehension starts with all of us knowing who and where we are. We don't, as a rule, make the opportunity to find out how we come across as individuals, with real people we deal with in the workplace, and usually we pretend the discomfort isn't there. We need to accept that there will be some discomfort. These topics are dangerous. People need to discuss dangerous topics with safe people first, and experiment with the results of their personal research in less predictable areas later. Feedback at a personal level is hard to elicit, and it may be painful – but it can be an investment. 'Working people' who live together could swap experiences. What makes them feel excluded? What kind of attitudes from men or women do they find least destructive and most motivating? What do they do about it? Men who are sceptical about, for instance, their own use of behaviour to imply dominance could consider asking women colleagues they trust how it comes across. Women could try playing less safe in order to push back the frontiers of expectation, enlarge the fund of knowledge, combat the stereotypes.

If men and women become more skilled at diagnosing and accepting the impact on one another of image, signals, styles of communication at work, they will reduce mutual incomprehension. When that is less distracting, both men and women can focus on the objectives of the job.

# 4 Measuring Up

Organisations have to keep changing to match – or, better, antici-
pate – new demands. For the peope who work in them, this
imperative ought to signify a first-class opportunity to experiment
with new ways of adding value, so that organisations can choose
the best of what's on offer. In practice, however, the capacity of
organisations to exploit original ideas is in double jeopardy. The
first hazard is that it may be hard for people to assess how they
should behave, against a range of sometimes conflicting organisational values and objectives during the process of change. Secondly, organisations may be using inappropriate yardsticks for the
measurement of merit, and therefore not only failing to identify
new sources of excellence, but downgrading whole populations of
people. Both these hazards – moving targets, inappropriate yardsticks – have serious implications for the integration of women into
the workplace.

## Moving Targets

Organisations are moving away from anachronistic systems and
hierarchies and hard autocratic values, which are no longer effective
in producing the required results, towards a focus on people, both
inside and outside organisations. Many companies are streamlining
their lines of communication and accountability so that their
structure is flatter, with far fewer levels between the chief executive
and the shop floor, with the aim of allowing messages to pass
quickly, personally and undiluted. Rather than simply expecting

people to follow instructions, organisations are working to 'empower' people to take personal responsibility. An emphasis on competition between individuals is being replaced by notions of partnership, teamwork and co-operation: working together to share the rewards.

Many organisations these days publicise a mission statement which acknowledges that the organisation is driven and shaped by more than the bottom line alone. Long gone (in theory, anyway) are the days when the Business Plan contained only quantitative financial targets and an outline of operational strategy to reach them. In the old days business was business and the rest of the world was irrelevant. Now we expect organisations to publicise their visions, values and priorities. These cover their attitudes towards people (employees, customers, suppliers) and their handling of issues such as accountability, communication, creativity and quality. It is also no surprise to meet statements of intent outlining a socially responsible corporate policy which might encompass topics as disparate as ethics, apartheid, cricket, sustainable forests, young people, AIDS, race and gender.

However, every organisation is at a different point in the process of change. There are still organisations which have hardly started re-examining their communications, and boast 'family trees' like triple-decker mangrove swamps, with roots and branches creeping upwards and downwards. Others display inconsistency in the messages they send out. One company, for instance, invested substantial sums on people-handling, team-building and strategic-thinking programmes for all its managers. The programmes emphasized the importance of consultation and ownership of decision-making processes. Six months into the programme a longish general memo about drainage was distributed to all its staff. The final item was the casual announcement of a decision to relocate Head Office forty miles away. Managers and staff had begun to accept that everybody had to contribute to revising the old routines; but the memo undermined their belief in the value of new styles of communication. Old habits have a long half-life, and stated commitment to new policies doesn't completely wipe out old-style behaviour. It may often seem more effective, more convenient and quicker to do things the old way. In yet other organisations, a

succession of rapid and far-reaching – and sometimes contra-
dictory – changes has been known to inspire a certain amount of
incredulity, not to say cynicism. 'We've learned to weather the
storms of corporate culture change. It's like water off a duck's
back.' New values are often seen more in the breach than the
observance.

Add to all this the overlay of gender, and confusion becomes
worse confounded. The old and the new become polarised. The old
hierarchical and autocratic style is characterised as 'masculine'. The
'macho management' style is held to account for the long-term
decline of worker satisfaction and productivity. Sharing and caring,
on the other hand, are portrayed as 'feminine' attributes which can
increase it. In *A Balanced Workforce?* published by the Ashridge
Management Research Group, a spokesman for the Henley Centre
for Forecasting was quoted as saying: 'We predict there will
continue to be, long-term, a feminisation of work, a move towards
the qualities women are seen to have in greater abundance than
men: team-working, intuitive skills and flexibility. They are perceived to have increasing value in a corporate context.' It's almost
as though organisations were being recommended to undergo a sex-
change operation.

With all this in mind, we need to look in more detail at some of
the aspects of changing priorities within organisations, and at how
men and women fare against the organisational ideal.

**The boss.** The profile of a leader is changing to match the new
demands on organisations. Portraying boss as hero is no longer
fashionable; it's less desirable and less effective to be seen as
winning battles, slaying enemies, commanding armies and moving
aggressively into new fields. Instead, the current 'ideal' boss is an
enabler, a facilitator, someone who seeks opportunities and gives
them to people to maximise, providing support and resource, but
also freedom to make mistakes and create individual initiatives.
Nevertheless, research suggests that people expect a boss to act
forcefully, sound confident and authoritative, have a high profile,
be emotionally stable, highly articulate and comfortable with

conflict, and always seem certain of the action that needs to be taken. In other words, a boss is still a stereotypical man.

Against this template, women often appear to fall short. Men are generally more popular as bosses. A survey of nearly 400 secretaries (whose sex we're not told, but can guess) was carried out in late 1991 by recruitment consultants Alfred Marks. It established that two out of three secretaries preferred to work for a man. Only 1 per cent said they would not be prepared to work for a man again. Male bosses, it seems, are much better at delegating. They are afflicted less by moods, and they don't interfere. It turns out also that secretaries will do more for men than for women, including services not strictly included in job descriptions, such as shopping, and making and changing social arrangements. Perhaps this is because men ask for such services more than women, who tend to be less comfortable about others ministering to them. Women bosses were much less popular. One in five of the secretaries in the survey who had worked for a woman said they would not be prepared to do so again. Female bosses, they thought, let their moods affect work more than men, and were less good at delegating. This may be because women are particularly conscientious, or just used to doing things for themselves.

Women's failure to delegate can be perceived as evidence of distrust and territorialism. Similarly, consultation can look like manipulation – a sin commonly attributed to women. If a boss has a notion of what she wants, trawls for other opinions, and then does the thing she'd first thought of, she can be perceived as a hypocrite, seeking input as a purely superficial exercise. In fact, it must make sense to give everyone's ideas an airing if they could conceivably elicit an ingenious alternative, and then, if they don't, revert to Plan A. Cynicism about women's motives and operational methods can creep in even at a high level. The Chairman of a very large company says: 'I love working with women. But I have a hunch that it's a female trait to attempt to manipulate. Men are pretty direct, but women do things by stealth – add a sentence, change a minute. It's the way they've achieved their results in the past – like putting money aside secretly from the housekeeping.' Women do things differently, but because men's ways are the norm, what women do can be perceived as bad, wrong or out of line – by women as well as men.

Women are much more of a focus for criticism than men, and the criticism individuals attract is very readily generalised to other women. It may be deserved, but even then it has a wider impact than comparable criticism of men. Paul Brack, Assistant Director of Finance with Croydon Borough Council, put it this way: 'I've known bad managers of both sexes. It's clear that at work a bad woman affects perceptions of all women, but a bad man doesn't tar all men with the same brush.' Another example: a male personnel director I met had clear views about women managers. What he might have said was something like this: 'Women often bring a fresh slant to proceedings – so fresh that it can disconcert other managers, who aren't quite ready to handle it. They often show a quick broad-brush grasp of situations. They have the courage to try things out even when they aren't positive of success, and they don't let masculine prejudice slow them down.' He might have done, but he didn't. His actual words were: 'Women managers take up quirky stances on subjects to press a point – gimmicks which misfire. They have too confident a belief that one set of circumstances can be translated to another situation; they need to master differences as well as similarities. They show a lack of humility in wanting to run before they can walk. Because it's a man's world, they think: "I'll show 'em!"' He did have some praise for women managers. 'Their value is in their intellect, social awareness, humanity, knowledge of fears and arguments. At their best, this makes them good negotiators.' Barrie Scott, an oil company manager for twenty years, thought that the promotion track itself could affect women managers. 'I like women in the workplace. I like the sense of humour and the chance to be risqué – but when women get to the top it's as though they've been reprogrammed and another chip put in. Every woman I've known in a middle to senior position has always lacked something. They try too hard; they become dogmatic and aggressive.' Research suggests that both men and women more readily see men as leaders; but more women will accept the notion that women can be effective leaders, too. There could be a simple reason for this: both men and women perform more like leaders when they are with members of their own sex. In one study women behaved most like leaders when they were with two other women: something men will never have seen, but women will.

Barrie Scott had noticed something else: 'Funny thing: women don't act aggressively and without humour when there are more of them. They become much easier to get on with.' Now, there's a thought to conjure with. There must come a point at which a critical mass is achieved, where women at a certain level suddenly seem part of the landscape so that their apparent faults fade out of the limelight. Again, it may be less to do with details of behaviour than with the social context. The majority presence of men affects the dynamics: research shows women achieve less, and are perceived more negatively, in male-dominated groups. When women make up more than half of any group, their contribution is rated more highly. When men are in the minority they aren't perceived negatively: a token man has a high status which makes his contribution desirable, even if he doesn't end up as the Little Red Rooster in the henhouse. On the whole, then, men tend to be more familiar with men as leaders in both mixed and single-sex groups, whereas women have experience both of men and women as leaders. This makes it hard for men to believe that women do things differently when men are not there. 'Women don't start jobs off,' said a male Detective-Constable. 'They wait to be told what to do.'

If their real strengths are not to remain forever elusive to men at work, women need to do what they do when men *are* there. This takes guts. Influence begets influence, but it has to start somewhere. Elizabeth Neville, Assistant Chief Constable of Sussex Police, told the story of her first big campaign, when she mobilised large numbers of police officers in a plan to contain the impact of a large, slow-moving Peace Convoy. She had to front the presentation to the squad, and brief a lot of men coherently in a short time. She chose a consultative approach, and found herself saying things like: 'Well, I've called you in for your expertise: what do *you* think?' The operation was a great success. Afterwards a senior colleague remarked: 'You went about that process in a very strange way.' 'Well, it worked, didn't it?' said Miss Neville. 'Mmm,' said the colleague, thoughtfully. 'He got a new idea out of that,' she says now. 'It was simply an experience he hadn't had before. It would have been far more difficult to get the chance to do it again if it hadn't turned out so well, though.' The price of earning respect as a female leader may be no second chance to make mistakes. The ultimate test of leadership style is effectiveness, and that was what Miss Neville appealed to when challenged.

Is it because of sex differences in leadership style that more women are not in positions of authority? Some of the research suggests male and female styles are different. Two American psychologists recently reviewed the research on how leaders emerge in groups which start without one. Some studies were laboratory-based, and some took place in real organisations. Overall, men were more likely to emerge as leaders. Men took over for short-term projects, and in groups carrying out tasks that did not require skilful people-handling; if people-handling was important, women were slightly more likely to lead the group. When people are observed in groups brought together for an experiment, there does appear to be a difference: women leaders tend to consult more readily, and men to direct. But the difference may be a function of the artificial nature of the experiment. When real male and female managers in an organisation are investigated, this difference does not appear so strongly – either because organisational roles override gender roles, or because both sexes are choosing the appropriate elements from both styles.

The perceived gender gap can be widened still further by a tendency to polarise the styles at extremes and label them firmly 'masculine' and 'feminine'. It can be limiting and misleading. Mrs Thatcher was caricatured as a man because she speaks forcefully and without consultation – in a stereotypically 'masculine' way. The Church, with its high premium on the 'feminine' value of loving thy neighbour, is nevertheless studded with men in all the positions of authority. It's not true that to do 'masculine' things you have to be – or behave like – a man, or that to do 'feminine' things you have to be – or behave like – a woman. People who conform closely to sex-typed behaviour find they reduce their ability to adapt to contingencies. They are more subject to disturbance than more flexible people, and less likely to generate innovative solutions. At times of change the extremes of 'masculine' and 'feminine' behaviour are restricting. Yet the cry for years has been:

'The only way to make it, girls, is by acting like a man.' The new message seems to be, albeit half-heartedly: 'Women have the qualities we need, chaps; achieve success by acting like a woman.' Yet everybody occasionally needs to be assertive, to invite people's involvement, to take the lead firmly at times of emergency, to offer a listening ear when someone is in trouble. For people of both sexes, picking the appropriate response off the entire range rather than feeling artificially confined to one end of it is a good way not only to work effectively but to weaken the stereotypes.

Many individuals can – and do – use both styles. It's this that leads to the concept of 'managerial androgyny' – the idea that the best managers use appropriate aspects of both 'masculine' and 'feminine' styles. Probably both men and women use different styles not only in different situations, but at different places on the organisational ladder. Elizabeth Neville says that she was much more conscious of the gender gap earlier in her career. When she was a Sergeant, the novelty was two-way: her men had never been supervised by a woman before. The more senior she has become, the less critical her gender, because: 'The power gulf replaces the sex gulf. My gender has become less important to me because my day-to-day dealings are more formal and less personal – or other things matter more.' When men and women are at equivalent rungs on the ladder, they may behave in a similar way. But because it's usually the less powerful positions which women fill, sex differences may appear significant.

It is a weakness in the research into gender and leadership style that it does not give indicators of effectiveness. Research is usually based squarely on self-perception, and not evaluated againt performance, which is difficult to arrange under experimental conditions. In organisations, however, effective performance does need to be measured objectively. This is far easier in terms of hard figures than soft values. 'There's loads of prejudice,' said a software marketing manager. 'But they can't argue with the figures, which show I've exceeded the targets.' Organisational values need to be translated into desirable results and standards of behaviour, and appropriately rewarded. If there is a mismatch between the values an organisation claims to espouse and the behaviour it rewards, then it will be desperately difficult for individuals to decide which style to cultivate. The 'masculine' style is conspicuous. The 'feminine' style is more self-effacing. If top people in organisations truly believe that the 'feminine' style has value too, then they have to find a way of making it clear what it's all about and who's doing it.

Both sexes need to be encouraged to use both styles effectively. Overall, the element of truth which sex stereotypes contain creates a balance of probability that, if there's a choice of behaviour, men will focus less on 'feminine' values than women. Measures of effectiveness tend to be higher and more stringent for women than for men. 'I'm ten times as good as my nearest male colleague,' said the software marketing manager, 'but I don't get the automatic respect that he does.' The male Personnel Director of a distribution company said: 'I'm afraid it's still true that women have to do better then men to gain the same consideration.' Not only do 'feminine' values need to be publicly supported, but also the women who use them effectively.

Organisations need aspects of both the 'masculine' and the 'feminine' styles. If the ship is on fire, holed and sinking it's not the moment to consult the crew and ask the Captain how she feels. But, if we must use the terms 'masculine' and 'feminine' at all, we should remember that they are shorthand; it doesn't really matter who does which, so long as there is a healthy interplay between the two, and both are recognised and valued for the benefit they bring, not rubbished for being out of kilter.

**The value of the posse.** Bill Cockburn, Chief Executive of the Post Office, says: 'I always used to be the Lone Ranger. It's only now I'm recognising the value of the posse.' Teamwork is taking a higher profile than ever before in many organisations. It demands co-operation, making the most of people's differing contributions, measuring group rather than individual achievement.

It's not easy to create an environment in which teams can consistently achieve high performance. In development workshops we try to illustrate the obstacles to solid teamwork by using management exercises. One exercise involves a set of building blocks and complete silence. Only one person has the power to touch the bricks. This person needs to communicate not only what they are doing and why, but also how the team will work together. One chap in this role regarded himself as the 'architect' of the tower, working to instructions from 'expert planners'. However, he failed to make this clear to the rest, who, distracted by his apparent executive power, thought of him as 'The Boss' and themselves as 'The Workforce'. He waited for advice and assistance from them, they waited for orders from him; everybody became confused and aggressive. They took twenty minutes to build the wrong-shaped tower, with manifest frustration and annoyance. If the roles of team members and the style of the leader are unclear – as often happens in reality in organisations where values are changing – mayhem can ensue.

Features which make high-performing teams successful include: clear goals and objectives; an emphasis on involvement, co-oper-ation, support and trust; open communication *and* confrontation; regular review of performance; a focus on individual development; a respect for the different approaches people bring to the task. Some of these features may need to be demonstrated for the inexperienced, and reinforced with a battery of evidence that they are effective and motivating. And because of the preconceptions that exist about the way women go about getting people to do what's necessary, teamwork as displayed by women may need to be upgraded twice over.

Another team exercise is so designed that benefits for all can be achieved quickly if everybody remembers the global objective and co-operates to achieve it, making sacrifices and giving ground in negotiation if required. There are plenty of opportunities for bluff and betrayal – which people generally take. Afterwards they see how they have mentally transformed a team task into a contest, which precludes honesty and the sharing of objectives – and they also tell, wryly, about precisely equivalent situations in the organ-isations they work for. If there are enough women to split the teams by gender, the exercise offers an interesting sidelight on prejudice. On one occasion, the women's team reneged on the deal they struck with the men's team. The men's leader stood up and berated them. He was tragic in his intensity. 'It's just like women! Dishonourable!

We made a deal! How could you do this!' He and his team aligned the women's behaviour with their gender and decided their worst fears were confirmed: women are devious, Machiavellian and not to be trusted. When a team composed entirely or mainly of men commits the same act of treachery during an exercise, the other team gets equally annoyed, but sex doesn't come into it. Disturbing results are attributed to the bad influence of Sales, or Engineering, or the personality of Southerners.

Because of its focus on relationships between people, the notion of teamwork is particularly likely to be attractive to women. Perhaps paradoxically, it can seem to men that women are not born to be team-players: not because they can't get on with other people, but because they lose their sense of the goal of the game. This may well be men's problem of perception. It's true that teams can get too cosy if they forget what they're constituted for, and sacrifice the objective in favour of the group unity. It's also true that women often spend considerable time building up the relationship between them. Some men misconstrue relationship-building as extraneous to the pursuit of the objective, rather than part of it, and therefore fear that women rate harmony higher than the goal. As for men in teams, the danger is that interdependence can seem like loss of status and autonomy.

If men and women are to be convinced that teamwork is of high value, involves interdependence and a respect for individuals, and that women have the skills to promote these elements and deploy them effectively, they need to be conscious of public successes like this one. In 1992, an eight-woman team beat 14 mixed teams to win the National Final of the Local Government Management Game in which a total of 150 local authorities competed. It involved a simulation exercise which demanded the solving of realistic and relevant issues in a hypothetical town. Rita Webb, Assistant Director (Public Affairs) at Birmingham City Council, was the leader of the winning team. Rita enjoys working with men, too, but says as a result of her experience that there are particular benefits in all-female teams. 'Women are incredibly versatile. They're competitive, but they eliminate the nasty bits. They manage competition without treading on each other's toes. For men, care and competition tend to alternate, whereas for women they can be concurrent. Women own up when they don't understand, where men might put up a bluff and leave people behind. On one issue most of us didn't have a clue, and we said so. If we hadn't owned up the whole issue would have been left with two people. As it was, we spread the load, and now all of us have a basic working knowledge. We did a lot of productive thinking as a collective, rather than allocating people to specialist areas – and I think that was the critical difference between us and the other teams. I agree it meant we duplicated much of the information in the short term, but longer-term it's meant that we have been able to pass it back to the Council much more widely. We felt confident, relaxed, and sure that each of us would give a high-quality performance. *And* there was no sexual harassment.'

**People people.** It must appear to many members of organisations that their leaders have their fingers crossed while they communicate the emphasis on people. One manager said: 'They're always saying people are important, but then they move on to something else. You can't trust the bastards.' One major service company invests serious money in a variety of people issues, and its Chairman recognises that fruitful relationships with its customers are vital for the bottom line, and that the key to creating and maintaining them is in the hands of his customer-facing champions, 98 per cent of them men. But, somehow, this message is not being received by the workforce. Something in the way they are treated within the organisation is at odds with the people-centred values which percolate from the top. Their sense is that their contribution to the success of the company is undervalued. It's a very confusing – and very common – apparent clash of values. In his book *Millennium*, about the challenges currently presented to organisations, management consultant Francis Kinsman tells the story of how 30 top managers, during a survey, each individually came up with the same signpost to the future, a message which he encapsulates as: People Matter Most. They were excited, elated and optimistic that the narrowing of the difference between business attitudes and private attitudes would help to solve tomorrow's business problems.

When some of them met subsequently to discuss the survey in which they had taken part, they spent the evening competing with one another. 'The 14 who attended abandoned the genuinely enlightened approach that characterised their original interviews, and opted instead for an exercise in verbal arm-wrestling – with a few exceptions who were quickly swept aside . . . a reversion to the schoolboy urge to be seen as the toughest kid on the block when all the other kids are around.' The mixed message comes out as: we need a focus on people and relationships, but it's wimpish and indeterminate to pursue them. Given this deep-rooted failure of those at the top to maintain a people-centred approach to business, no wonder men and women in organisations are unsure about its continuing value.

Even when people not only accept that the key to the future lies in excellent people-handling but try to cultivate it, the way men and women set about the task shows differences in approach. These were exemplified for me at one workshop I ran on selection interviewing. Delegates were asked to role-play appropriate scenarios with a professional actor, observed by the rest of the small group. I saw two consecutive role-played interviews, the first led by a woman called Dora. The 'applicant' – Nicky – was an actor who had been briefed to portray a particular personality and reveal a fictional life history. Dora had prepared probing questions for her, but in the event Nicky spent 90 per cent of the time nattering away while Dora dropped in an occasional 'Oh, really?' or a 'How did you feel when that happened?' Nudge, nudge, nudge and manoeuvre. By the end of the session Dora had answers to all her questions, but had actually framed only a fraction of them. The information had flowed quite naturally from what was effectively a two-way chat about the job, the applicant and the prospects. A considerable amount of ostensibly 'redundant' data emerged, including the colour of Nicky's leotard and the habits of her dog. Dora ended up happy that she had enough information to make the decision.

Stephen held the second interview. He ran through all his questions – again, skilfully compiled – one by one. There was no small talk, no connection between the topics. When Nicky volunteered information beyond the strict requirements of the question,

Stephen took no notice until he reached that topic on his agenda. He treated the session as an inquisition in which it was Nicky's obligation to respond effectively to what he asked. Many leads Nicky gave were lost. By the time Stephen finished, he too was satisfied that he had enough information to make his decision.

When we discussed the two interviews as a group, we all agreed that both performances had elicited the right sort of information. But the room was divided by gender on the comparative value of, on the one hand, friendliness, and, on the other, control. The debate made it clear that 'successful people-handling' meant two different things to women and men. All the women thought Stephen had been cold, unfriendly and offputting, had done nothing to make the job seem any more than a bunch of technical tasks, and had undermined any enthusiasm Nicky might have had. The men were astounded at this. They thought Stephen had managed the interview very well, and fully succeeded in making it clear that he was the boss. The men also thought Dora had completely lost control of the interview, and had therefore compromised her status as manager. She had allowed Nicky to guide the process, and it had seemed more like an informal gossip than a proper business-like introduction to a new prospective job. 'The trouble with women,' said one delegate, 'is that they think relationships are more important than results.' The women were amazed that obvious managerial status should be of such consequence. The relationship Dora had so quickly built had, they thought, *ensured* a useful result, not *replaced* it. Whereas the men needed to see that someone was in charge, the women were supporting another model for 'control', in which a partnership could be quickly established, and then create its own momentum in achieving an appropriate conclusion.

Both men and women can deal one to one with others superbly well and appallingly badly. But the styles they use can look very different; and they often disagree fundamentally on yardsticks for 'success'. It is unfortunate for women if an advanced skill is interpreted as an example of unmanaged chaos. It's the mixture as before: confusing messages in the workplace about a value which is supposed to be significant, and in practice different interpretations of how to turn that value into action.

**Ethics.** 'Ethics' is a Nineties buzzword. It's not that they never existed before in the business world; but currently companies are formalising their attitudes in guidelines for behaviour. The quest for integrity can be tacit, or encapsulated in a mission statement. One Managing Director chose to explain to his employees face to face why he was introducing a new statement of values to the company: 'Most transactions are cut and dried, and it's clear what should be done, both commercially and morally. If the course of action is not clear and there could be a conflict between commercial and moral objectives, knowing the company values will help you as individuals make a decision which the company can support. I hope you will find that these company values echo your own.'

While the principles of honesty, integrity, loyalty are equally likely to be found in men's and women's personal value systems, there may be differences in what they mean by them. Two sets of research suggested that men and women approach moral issues in different ways. The psychologist L. Kohlberg produced a now classic series of moral dilemmas on which he asked people to comment. One was the story of a man called Heinz, whose wife was dying for lack of a drug which was impossibly expensive. Should Heinz steal the drug from the druggist who was charging this outrageous price? Most men decide that the overriding principle is that the right to life takes precedence over the right to property. Women tend to respond with further questions about Heinz, the wife and the druggist. From the responses which he collected, Kohlberg concluded that there are stages of moral judgment which we pass through as we mature. Some of us get stuck at infantile levels, where decisions may be based on the best way of avoiding trouble. The ultimate in maturity, he said, is the adoption of abstract principles of justice: and men reach this point more readily than women. In her book *In a Different Voice* Janet Gilligan followed up his research. She felt that Kohlberg's league-table devalued the mature judgement of women, which rests on an assessment of responsibility and the human dimension of particular cases. Her conclusion was that there are two equally valid ways of judging the right thing to do – and that they are different.

Men filter general rules out of particular instances. The key to women's solutions of moral dilemmas is empathy: what would that feel like, where have I met something like that before? For women, circumstances alter cases. So, while both men and women may support an organisation's mission and values in principle, there are likely to be differences in their evaluation of what they see happening to people in practice.

Often women don't like what they see. The high moral tone of an organisation may not be reflected in its day-to-day transactions. Often transactions are more like political games, with their own rules, disconnected from any ethical principles promoted by the company, driven by expediency. One manager, who had watched a variety of Financial Directors in the throes of negotiation, said: 'Men use bullshit, persuasion without logical basis, personal views, opinions. Senior women are phenomenal – despite the pressure on them, they're better equipped with facts.' The Director of a multi-national company found women's different approach an unnecess-ary element in a system which, he feels, is already working perfectly well. 'Women are more honest and less political. Men enjoy being beastly to each other in meetings, and have fun pulling the wool over each other's eyes – yes, it's the bullshit factor . . . Women might bring a greater breadth of view, different experience, a different view on people, but we don't need it. I suppose discussion might be more rigorous with more women about, but I don't believe we are missing anything.' A male Detective-Constable damned with faint praise: 'Women are more honest. They're less creative and they don't take short cuts.' At the same time he lamented the public's current disapproval of a profession which 'used to be honourable 25 years ago', presumably before too many police officers took too many short cuts and were found out.

Many women get the strong impression that the focus on people, principles and good citizenship is a fair-weather policy; a motto for the airy reaches of the Boardroom, not for the dust and sweat of the operational arena; a public relations slogan for gaining commer-cial credibility rather than an honest framework for operational deeds. The important thing for many men is the game. They think that people who can't or won't play are unrealistic and not much fun. The justification for their position is that politics are part of business, and that women just don't understand how the wheeling and dealing contribute to the business objective. It's one of the reasons why an open display of emotions is out. As in poker, it doesn't do to be transparent when you're fighting for the best deal you can get. Women, on the other hand, feel that games undermine people. A marketing manager in a computer software company reduced her ambitions precisely because of this. 'When I started on this path I was thinking: "I want to be a career woman and get to the top and no one shall stop me." Now I don't want to be at the top. They're a load of shits with the wrong values. My perception of them has changed. The way they treat people works for them, but I'm not interested in being like that.' The slogans may be newly minted, but the standards may not have caught them up; and the mismatch may be more significant for women.

The first part of the double jeopardy which prevents organisations from getting the best from their people is the combination of general and specific misunderstandings: general misunderstandings about the worth of 'old' and 'new' types of values and behaviour; specific misunderstandings about the way men and women display them. Men performing in a 'masculine' way are comprehensible, comfortable, validated by history. Anybody performing in a 'feminine' way needs to explain what they are doing, so as to establish credibility for new types of behaviour, and sidestep incomprehension and frustration. In addition, women have to counteract a legacy of negative attributions. Organisations need to make it crystal-clear what they expect and what they will reward.

## Inappropriate yardsticks

The key to successful organisations lies in assessing merit wherever it appears, according to clearly established criteria, and this is where the second part of the double jeopardy starts. Wilfully, or through ignorance, organisations often reinforce, rather than demolish, barriers which prevent merit from being achieved, recognised and rewarded. People make their way in organisations by submitting themselves to tests and ordeals, judged by people who have passed that way before. When the norm is masculine, and times are changing, the judges, their methods and their yardsticks may not properly take account of innovation and difference. Decision-makers often play safe. 'Snap!' they cry. 'Let's find something which matches what we've had before.' This occurs at all decision points in organisations, from entry of a new applicant onwards. What they've had before is often men. It takes a bold and visionary decision-maker to see merit in something which deviates from a known pattern.

The final decisions on selection and promotion are taken by people, on the basis not only of 'objective' fact, but of intangibles such as fit, liking, balance. Who judges? Men, mostly, since it is they who are at the top of most organisations. An assessment consultant was blunt about the outcome. 'There are bigots every-where – but a bigot in the local office is less dangerous than a bigot at HQ.' A Personnel Director felt that secret bigots might be more of a threat. 'What I'm afraid of is that prejudice may still be there, but driven underground by people like me shouting for equality of opportunity.' Prejudice is not confined to men. An Institute of Management report published in November 1992 disclosed that nearly one man in five surveyed said they found it difficult to work for a woman – and so did more than one woman in ten. Only two-thirds of the women surveyed felt their male bosses showed enough respect, and over a quarter did not feel they gained enough respect from female superiors. Women who make it do not necessarily help others to do so – a phenomenon often described as the 'Queen Bee' syndrome.

The chief method of selection is undoubtedly interview, with or without additional, more objective tools. At interview individual weighs up individual, sometimes instantly. All the professional, social and sexual hiccups already described may come into play at this point, and unleash highly damaging prejudices and unfounded assumptions – at sight.

A cartoon appeared on our office notice-board one day. In somewhat cynical fashion it depicts two interview candidates – a man and a woman – as they might appear to their (male) assessor. The man sits, legs firmly apart, grim-faced and uncompromising. The interviewer's thought-bubble reads *An OK person, putative father, future breadwinner.* The candidate's stance is aggressive.

*Firm decision-maker.* He apparently has an undistinguished BSc. *I think we can afford to be generous here.* He has a chesty girlfriend. *Look good at next company do.* He demands two months' leave and incentives. *Knows what he wants.* His mental processes seem a trifle pedestrian. *Slow but sure.* He's unimaginative. *Logical.* He's obviously clumsy. *He'll have a go, though.* He's wearing socks like the interviewer's. *Instant feeling of empathy.* He's wearing a tie like the interviewer's. *Good dress sense.*

The other candidate sits relaxed. She's a woman. *Off to have babies then demanding maternity leave and creche facilities.* She's smiling. *Come-on?* There's a handbag by her chair. *Not masculine enough for a working environment.* She speaks assertively. *Aggressive.* She talks of her ambitions. *Pushy.* She's not wearing make-up. *Lesbian? Feminist?* The top button of her blouse is undone. *Cheap?* She's obviously informed, aware, effective. *Unfeminine.* Her skirt is of decorous length. *Not enough leg.* She looks at ease. *Too cocky by half.* She's neat-fingered. *Fit for women's work.* Her speech is clear and direct. *Comes on strong.* She's articulate. *Too cocky by half.* She seems confident. *Castrator.* Some of her answers are intuitive. *Illogical.* She has a PhD. *Too cocky by half.*

Yes, it's overdone – but many would give wry acknowledgment that there's a basis of reality to it. A female selector, however bigoted, would be less likely to be personally affected by length of skirt or the threat of castration. What any selector needs to do, however, is to concentrate on skills and competencies rather than allow assumptions to set the frame.

Interviews are best backed up by other, less impressionistic methods of assessment. Biographical data is one. A woman is forgiven more easily than a man for possessing a work history with holes in it; but it may not present as convincing a case to decision-makers as a classic complete masculine work record. For selection or promotion to management roles, simulation exercises may be used. Generally they involve short-term projects – solving a problem against a deadline, for instance – which reflect men's style more naturally, so research suggests. Such exercises don't test the ability to create productive long-term relationships, which are a much more significant ingredient in the way work is actually carried out in organisations, and which are women's forte. Other simulations may involve social dynamics. For instance, in a debate in which a number of candidates are involved, the chances are that sex ratio will affect outcomes of the test: in a group of mostly men, it's unlikely that a woman will assume leadership. Unless assessors are fully aware of the implications of social dynamics, they may make misleading judgments which ignore the result of group interaction. The result is a series of self-fulfilling prophecies. The artificial environment of many exercises ignores female strengths and tests women to destruction on masculine ones.

In addition, various filters which let men through keep women out. The Civil Service closely monitors the position of women. Women comprise about half the applicants for posts as administrative trainees – but only just over a quarter of those accepted. The *average* test scores for men and women are the same, but the *highest* scores are gained by men. Acceptance is contingent on a high pass mark on the tests. Whatever additional strengths women may offer, the pass mark automatically cuts more of them out. Age limits for entry affect women more than men, because of the greater likelihood that women will have taken time out for family reasons.

Of course, the pendulum can swing too far the other way. So bold and innovative does an organisation aim to be that it overestimates the quality of a woman applicant. This can set women up for failure if the measure is unreachable; and it creates a false benchmark for achievement by women. We need to avoid overcompensating by overestimating women as winners. We also need to ensure that organisations pay attention to solid merit at less than the very highest levels. The Personnel Director of Royal Mail: 'Highflyers are sexier than junior managers, and there's an overconcentration on them. We should begin to accept that hungry superambition is not the only thing we need to foster – and in any case it has a good chance of looking after itself.'

Items demanded of a potential applicant for employment or promotion will include commitment, and may exclude women on the grounds that they don't have enough of it, because of family demands. A senior Personnel Director was blunt about this assumption: 'Women are not necessarily dedicated to their employer. Men go for continuity, women for slugs of money.' The most significant point here is that decision-makers can assume that it is career breaks and motherhood which cause women to be less qualified and therefore less likely to be selected. But, says Dr Wendy Hirsh, co-author of *Women into Management*, 'Women fall behind in their careers long before they become mothers.'

Why? A number of misleading assumptions about women's achievements affect their chances of reaching higher levels in organisations. To become an expert at any skill, you need three things: numerous chances to experiment, plus the luxury of making mistakes; trustworthy comment from observers to enable you to make realistic judgments about your own performance; and suf-ficient information. If you can rely on these, the progression from Novice (watching others and performing by rote) to Competent Exponent (doing a good routine job) to Expert (giving something extra in a new situation) becomes smoother. However, several factors in the workplace conspire to diminish all three of these indispensable conditions as far as women are concerned.

The first factor is the notion of A Woman's Place. Women tend to be confined to areas where experiment is limited: service and nurturing occupations, and support functions. A woman doing 'women's work' has plenty of female role-models to observe, except, probably, at the highest levels; so the pattern will tend to repeat itself.

'Men's work' covers far more options and creates far more varied experience. The learning process is very different for male and female novices here. When breaking new ground, a female novice carries far less automatic authority than a man: witness the male medical students who are addressed as 'Doctor', while females are called 'Nurse'. Nobody deserves authority, in the end, unless they earn it – but it saves energy if they can start with an assumption which they can grow into. Novices of both sexes generally have a selection of male experts to observe and imitate. However, where a male novice can take over certain kinds of behaviour without much thought, a woman has to translate them into something which looks natural and appropriate when she performs them. Say a male manager enters an office where three people are working. He claps the first chap on the back, puts an arm round the second as he hands him a report to re-write, and delivers a lengthy instruction to the third without preamble. The watching novice may decide that this was a brilliant bit of team-building, worth emulating. The clap on the back conveyed solidarity and cheer; the arm round the shoulder communicated encouragement and sympathy to compensate for the tedium of the re-write; and the instruction demonstrated knowledge and leadership. But if the novice is a woman she can't just copy the behaviour. She needs to analyse why and how the manager's activities worked, and then seek the nearest feminine equivalent. She can't touch the men without ambiguity, and so has to find an alternative – perhaps a form of words. Since lectures are rarer and less welcome from women than men, she'll have to dress the instruction up a bit, and she may achieve more effective results if she can get the man to tell *her* what should be done. Whether the novice is male or female, personality will, of course, also affect the result. But a woman needs to be more creative; it may take her ten experiments to find a viable formula, whereas a male novice can usually learn directly from observation of a role model.

All this creates a vicious circle. Women may appear to learn less than men from projects which they are involved in – so women don't get allocated to projects – so they often don't get extra chances to learn. But if they do? If some open-minded manager decides to take a risk, lets a woman have a go, and focuses on the positive aspects of her performance, having given her the confidence of managerial support, and communicated a strong expectation (and indeed hope) of being surprised by the result? With that kind of backing and opportunity, a woman can steer clear of traditional and perhaps restricted solutions to old problems, and she can take from existing role models as much as she needs and no more. She can bring a fresh vision, illuminated by her different balance of skills (especially understanding and getting more out of relationships) and her competence in understanding multiple aspects of a task simultaneously. She can be inventive, and she can focus on positive results rather than the difficulties of getting there.

The second major factor which can hinder women's progress is any sort of weakness in the feedback loop. Feedback is most valuable when it's part of an ongoing dialogue, reinforced by formal procedures such as the appraisal process, and followed by specific training to address shortfalls which have been identified.

Formal appraisal is a much-misunderstood process at the best of times, and much of the research shows that women are treated in a different way from men. A report funded by the Equal Opportunities Commission and published in 1992 by the Institute of Manpower Studies highlighted unintentional discrimination against women because of poorly designed performance appraisals and the use of subjective targets. Male managers value the male stereotype – dynamism, assertiveness, motivation, ambition. Female managers value flexibility, perceptiveness, honesty. If men dominate management, these perceptions influence the decisions which are made, and men are more likely to get promotions and training. Other research suggests that men are more likely to receive direct criticism which enables them to focus their effort to improve. Women are more likely to receive general reassurance without detail. Perhaps appraisers underestimate women's need. Perhaps they are sparing themselves embarrassment. A middle manager in a large retail organisation said: 'Men are much easier to deal with. Women take things so personally. I don't like to give too much criticism, because she gets so upset.' He should re-assess his need to feel comfortable; it is stopping him giving his female staff the value they are entitled to expect, and perhaps shortening their potential career path. The women should put the strength of their reaction in context, by making it clear that it reflects the high importance to them of identifying ways of improving their performance.

Managers who undertake appraisals with women need to combat the risk of self-fulfilling prophecy, by including expectations of unexpected achievement, and by expressing certainty, rather than doubt, in order to encourage confidence. They should also identify their assumptions about women – and then re-examine them, to ensure they are not penalising individuals.

Large, quality companies take pride in the training they offer, but their faith in it may be over-optimistic unless it takes account of gender differences. Many jobs are rendered even more complex by having to be done in company with, or by means of, other people. For instance, a woman who attends a meeting with six men will have to adopt completely different strategies from a man in a parallel situation. The professional objective may be the same, but the social and sexual undercurrents won't be. The format of training matters, too. Training is often arranged at distant locations for days at a time, so that the course has to be residential. There are enormous benefits in residential workshops, but not if they filter out people with a strong commitment to be at home at the end of a working day.

A third factor which seriously impedes women's performance is the difficulty they experience in gaining all the information relevant to their job. For instance, a major brewery is proud of its Equal Opportunities activities, and also of the way its area managers work as a team across its territory. In practice, teamwork is co-ordinated by after-hours sessions in the brewery's pubs, when the chaps get together and sort things out. The women area managers do not see this as an equal opportunity. They can't fulfil the job adequately without it; yet a networking meeting masquerading as a night out with the boys is nowhere itemised on their job descriptions.

A senior Finance Manager: 'We set up a really important meeting last Tuesday, to start at 6, but at 5.30 all the women got up and went home. Unbelievable.' If it was that important, why was it not on company time?

The Personnel Director of a very large company: 'What women don't get enough of is information – the political stuff that runs organisations. Effective performance and chances of promotion require you to know the soft and the strong parts of your superiors, and those are the things women miss out on, by not being there when that information is being shared.' Aha. Vital secrets are *not* included on formal agendas, but tossed around at the periphery? Judgments are *not* objectively based on results? Promotion *does* depend on who you know? This seems to give the lie to any claim that people are being assessed solely on merit.

Worse, there's the Club. For some, it's a Boy's Club – relatively harmless, a place where testicles can be scratched with impunity, and nobody needs to worry about not being transcendentally grown-up. (One female manager feelingly described the leitmotiv of meetings with a colleague in the early days of implementing their Equal Opportunities programme: 'It was very off-putting: he was forever adjusting his masculinity.') For others, it's a more serious affair, and *very* exclusive. Its members powerfully oppose the entry of women, because they are women. One Director felt strongly about it. 'I don't understand,' he said, 'why ladies *want* to join the Men's Club.' 'What's that?' said I. 'Well, places where men do what they do – like sports clubs, the Church of England, the Boards I sit on, where men understand the politics. Ladies behave differently, they drink different things, they don't drop fag-ends on carpets. It wouldn't be the same with ladies in it. Ladies prevent it working properly. Why do they want to join the Church, a declining institution, moribund and stagnant? Why don't they make their own institutions? Why don't they set up their own Church? The Club is part of the success of the company objective. Losing it would diminish the company.' We can argue about the virtues of having single-sex leisure activities like sports clubs; but it's frightening to hear the notion of 'club' expressed as a synonym for work in general. And could the Church be stagnant because there aren't enough women directing it?

If the real work is done and the important information spread in some cosy enclave independent of company structure, what price equal opportunity? The Institute of Management report published in November 1992 disclosed that 43 per cent of respondents nominated the Men's Club as the chief cause of women's failure to make faster headway. Increasingly women are learning to network, though their institutions are far less powerful than those of the men. However, so strong is their distaste for the Men's Club that some women often deliberately don't join anything that might look like its female equivalent, so as not to shut out men by creating a mystery in-group. One City woman said: 'I suppose I connive at their comfort by not joining ladies' luncheon clubs.'

Women call for access to everything they need to be effective. They don't want to spoil anyone's fun or be a wet-blanket, but they do need every piece of information which first-class performance requires. Without it their achievement can only fall short.

## Unequal results

The same yardstick is ostensibly used for men and women, but is creating unequal opportunities. Behind the scenes women are not getting the exposure, the practice, the information they need. The catch is that the shortfall may be underestimated by both women and their judges. It is difficult for women to diagnose why an activity didn't work: because it was badly performed, because it was performed by a woman, because it was misinterpreted or sabotaged by men, or because it was a rotten idea in the first place? Confidence takes a knock, because progress is slow and painful. 'Women are slower to learn than men,' confided a senior manager in one large group. It becomes personal: the woman's 'fault' she's not achieving, a personality deficiency rather than the result of situations created by men. Even supportive men are only useful up to a point, because their experience is also limited. They may be reduced to generalisations such as: 'Believe in yourself!' – but they can't give a straightforward recipe for visible achievements which will shore up self-belief.

Because of men's misinterpretations women have to experiment more; because most of the models are masculine, divergences from them will be called 'mistakes' by men; because of men's judgments (or misjudgments) women will need to use up valuable time and emotional reserves in analysing and coming to terms with the results of their experiments. No wonder many women are hesitant about applying for promotion. Their goals may be identical to men's, but in a man's world they are further away, take longer to get to and cost more in pain and self-doubt.

If women are the equals of men in competence and ability they'll make it, won't they? Not if the rules are slanted, the judges biased or blinkered, the processes misunderstood, the objectives garbled, and the participants confused about the results they are expected to achieve.

The system may look as though the opportunities it offers are equal, but at every turn there is potential for confusion in establishing the benchmarks for success, and for injustices in assessing men and women against them. Women provide an exciting new balance of skills, but they may be judged as failed men, or something strange and dangerous – something which at best can be moulded into a shape that just about fits the organisation. If organisations want innovation they should provide space for experiment, by re-assessing their values, welcoming 'mistakes' – and learning a less repressive terminology for behaviour which diverges from the norm. It's a risk, but without it all they can expect is conservatism and stagnancy.

# 5 Roles: Big world, Small world, Real world

What happens outside work impinges on what happens in it. There aren't two separate populations: workers, and people who live detached from work. We'd look silly if there were: nobody providing goods or services would have a clue about their customers. Organisations don't employ robots programmed solely to do the tasks outlined on their job description. They employ complete people, with ambitions, fears and hopes beyond the nine-to-five, for whom work is only one item on the agenda. When the day's task is done, men and women go home, and have to make sense of life with their other halves, their friends, their parents, their children. People play roles upon different stages. The most effective people fit their roles comfortably, and move easily from one to the other. Both individuals and organisations can benefit by – or suffer from – the crossover between the Big World of work and the Small World of home.

This chapter lays out some of the implications of that crossover. The first part is an account of the difficulties men and women encounter as they try to operate effectively across the two worlds. The second part looks at how organisations deal with the impact of non-work roles on working life.

## Individuals and the crossover

It used to be so simple, once. Back in the old days – up to, say, thirty years ago – men expected to be breadwinners and women to be breadwinners' wives. The breadwinner used to go out to work, and his wife looked after the house and the children. The nuclear family unit made a lot of sense as a way of survival. The deal was that one adult contributed money, and the other dedicated time. Between them they serviced all family members, including the next generation who were not yet ready to contribute. Men – explorers and inventors, possessors of physical strength to enable them to build and steer – provided the action. Women – nurturers and carers, interested in people, nimble-fingered, with a prodigious capacity for rendering order out of chaos – provided the glue which bound the family unit together.

At least everyone knew where they were. Phrasebooks to guide dialogue between parallel worlds were not necessary; what people had was a script. Men were the masters of the Big World, and dictated the parameters for women in the Small World. I was taught in the Fifties and Sixties to make the best of what I was going to get. There's hidden power in sacrifice, I learned; it's only realistic to expect personal goals to be frustrated, since you can't have it all; satisfaction is to be found in living through your man and your children; woman is the power behind the throne, the quietly influential matriarch, facilitating activity but not taking part in it. To do this, I learned, it's vital for the woman to be at home, knitting it together, not departing for far horizons and leaving the household to fend for itself. Excursions into the workplace were therefore expected to be of secondary importance to me, as to many women, both personally and financially. All I wanted was a man, a baby and a job which fitted school holidays. At that time there was little problem about what to wear, what kind of behaviour was appropriate, what to teach boys and girls to prepare them for their future. Organisations did not have procedures in place to ensure equal opportunities, because the Big World was for men anyway. As a coherent system for a population of Breadwinners and Their Wives, it was first-class.

Except for many of the women involved, for whom the system was a bit of a consolation prize. It took the Women's Movement in the late Sixties and Seventies to awaken women – and men – to the idea that such a system was asymmetrical, wasteful, unfair and avoidable. So, from the early Seventies, the 'Breadwinner and His Wife' system began to be shaken up by women's insistence on more balance in relationships.

There were other family formats, of course. In 1969 sociologists

Rhona and Robert Rapoport were the first to investigate families in which both adults were following a career – less common then than it is now. They distinguished three main difficulties. Couples suffered from overload: without someone in a dedicated support role there was suddenly a lot for both to do on top of the daily work routine. In addition, these couples were out of step with the expectations of society, and had to find some way of coping. Thirdly, the individuals concerned also had to identify what it meant to them to be the male or female partner in a domestic set-up which was no longer based on tradition. If these new stresses could be resolved, the Rapoports had high hopes for a future based solidly on a constructive interplay between home and work. The outcome would be more fulfilling domestic partnerships and family relationships, *and* a workforce in which both men and women would balance their lives fully and be able to reach equally high positions. A Brave New World, indeed.

And so it was, back in 1972, that my partner and I started our joint life, under the dual influences of the masculine Breadwinner Syndrome and the Feminist Movement. The first affected us strongly, the second subliminally. Since then I've been: married childless earner, jobless housewife and mother, single parent of two, main breadwinner in family of four, and joint breadwinner. My partner Chris has been: married childless earner, main bread-winner, weekend father, self-employed, unemployed and joint breadwinner. In fact, we've tried almost every permutation two people can achieve – and never got it right.

I wouldn't claim that our life as a couple has been altogether typical. Periods of employment were punctuated by acquiring, expanding and selling a small business; married life was terminated by divorce and succeeded by living in sin. We've also been blessed with options not open to all. The sale of our business gave us enough cash to regroup and retrain, and the freedom to consider sending our boys away to school. But, with hindsight, we see that many of our experiences mirror variations on managing the cross-over (and, especially, failing to manage it) which are becoming increasingly common in the workplace.

Anyway, what's typical, these days? Only seven households in a hundred contain Breadwinner, wife and family. Only one in four contain two parents and dependent children. Marriage and remarriage are in steep decline, and we have the highest divorce rate in Europe. One child in four is born out of wedlock. One-parent families are on the increase, and one household in four consists of just one person. In just over half of all couples with children, both adults work. In 1982, 58 per cent of women worked outside the home. Ten years later, the figure was 68 per cent. The figures for mothers working were 49 per cent in 1981, 59 per cent in 1991. Six million people, of whom nearly three in five are women, look after old or disabled relations. Both the workplace and the home are far more complex places in which to operate than they were even ten years ago, largely because of the way they are linked. Every single one of these domestic combinations implies a different set of dynamics which all those involved have to cope with. Pressures can be substantial, painful and sometimes incomprehensible.


**Childless working couple.** When Chris and I were a childless working couple, twenty years ago, the incomes were fine, the responsibilities were joint and could be fitted into convenient corners, and the only real fly in the ointment was my own lack of freedom to go for jobs that suited me. But I accepted that – for, as Chris used to say in those days: 'Eventually I will have to support you, so we should make sure my career is one that will let me do it properly.' We didn't suffer from the problems the Rapoports identified of being out of step with society, because I had every intention of becoming a full-time wife and mother when the time came. We had friends, and we had jobs; inevitably what suffered was the household, and the biggest rows we had were over housework and money. They were classics: he thought I should do more and spend less; I thought it was a bit much to expect me to do more than half the housework when I was working too. Chores were a source of friction then, and have remained so for nearly twenty years, no matter what role either of us was fulfilling. It's only in the last three or four that we've achieved a more laid-back stance. Chris says: 'My perception has always been that I've done more chores than you. You have different priorities.' I reply: 'You've done much more than many men do – but what you do has

value because you're a man, and what I do doesn't because women
are supposed to do it.'

Housework is the rock on which many relationships founder,
even now. Many women still try to do it all, whatever their working
status; they still take prime responsibility for an unequal share of
the domestic load. Reasons women give for doing housework are
that they feel personally responsible, or fear the tasks won't get
done otherwise. Men regard external maintenance as their responsibility, so they'll paint drainpipes and dig the garden. They'll deal
with transformations and major projects, such as decorating a
room. Anything else they do is for their partner's benefit: 'I help
her with the washing-up'; 'I tidied the bedrooms for her.' Housework still belongs to women. A European Commission Survey
published in August 1922 reported that British men did less
housework than other Europeans. Seventy-four per cent said they
would not take responsibility for domestic chores. If the family
employs domestic help, it's usually the woman who organises it,
and it's regarded as a perk for her rather than a service to the
family. I mentioned the phrase 'gender issues' to one businessman.
He immediately jumped to the conclusion that my line was that
men should do more at home. 'My God,' he said, 'talk about role
reversal – I'm chauffeuring for two, cleaning, and cooking dinner
for eight while she goes off horse-riding . . . The trouble is,
whatever men do, it's never enough. What more do women want?'
There is constant pressure on the woman and a source of conflict
within the family, if the underlying assumption is that she does
chores by statute, and others do them as a favour.

Ask any couple which of them does the ironing. Nine times out
of ten it's the woman. Ironing is not just a chore, but a touchstone.
It's amazing how often it comes up as a sticking-point during
discussions about the difficulties of dealing with the demands of
different roles. Nowadays Chris does his own ironing, and I do
mine, and we both do a proportion of the joint stuff, unless one of
us is very busy. Both our boys do their own. This seems to be very
unusual. If I tell people about it I can see them thinking (sometimes
simultaneously) – 'Well, she's got it right/she's not performing her
duties/what a wimp her man must be/what a life her boys must
lead, poor little devils/it's not right/I'm glad I don't have to do

that.' At fourteen my elder son asked plaintively while he washed up and I dried: 'Why aren't you a typical mother?' 'What's that?' I replied. 'Somebody who does *all* their children's ironing and has a job in a library two days a week.' At fifteen he said, as he sewed the name-tape on his fifth pair of boxer shorts while his younger brother cooked supper for four, 'I understand this is my responsibility, but I wouldn't have minded some help.' Have I taught them valuable independence, or stolen precious childhood moments they can never get back? I guess none of us will know for another twenty years.

Another theme permeated those early years which certainly isn't peculiar to us. Chris says: 'I was jealous of your work colleagues. I resented your attention to them all. I felt I had a prior claim on you and they were competing for time, action, sexual interest. So I separated myself from it. I didn't want to get involved with it. I hated being asked to your work functions.' It's far from uncommon for men to underplay the importance to their wives of their wives' careers, but to expect their own careers to be of paramount significance. Men and women value different kinds of support from their other halves. What women value more is emotional, financial and chore support from their spouse. But they often don't get it. A marketing manager divorced her husband a couple of years after she had returned to the workplace when her youngest child was about three. 'I spent years helping him to build up his career, giving him backing and moral support. But he wouldn't help me with mine. He didn't believe I could do it. I was only real to him when I was washing up.' Research suggests that it matters less to men that their wives have a job than to women that their men do. This could be a covert status contest, in which the man quietly ensures that his own occupational commitment outweighs his wife's – or simply a throwback to the old Breadwinner syndrome.

Men expect their women to identify with their husband's career, and the women sometimes resent the imbalance. A Director of one large firm recounted the splash his wife had made when she attended her first company Christmas dinner. The way he told it, it was a joint triumph. She interrupted: 'I feel as though all I am is the boss's appendage.' Pleased as she was with his pride in her, it rankled suddenly that the highly successful creative professional and mother of two had sunk to something about the level of a handbag.

**Breadwinner and his wife and family.** Our next episode had Chris as sole earner and new father, and Pat as housewife and mother. This was to have been the culmination of my dreams, hopes and desires. I wanted to create a warm, loving environment for four people. My ambition was to give my kids the best I could, which to me meant giving them my full-time presence. I wanted to bandage knees, watch eyes shine at Christmas, ride in a puffa-train and tell two small boys all there was to know about moo-cows. Be there, see it all, interpret the world, make it safe.

I did those things. I also found myself spending the day doing chores while the babies were asleep, and the evening clamouring for attention from somebody who seemed to think his only duty was reluctantly to hand over the housekeeping cheque. Housework was interminable. Meals took hours to prepare and minutes to eat. The only way to gain any fulfilment out of life at all was to see the role as infinitely more glorious than its component tasks. Taking grime off collars is sublime if it's a vital, though subordinate, contribution to the real stuff of life. But it was no good if the only person who thought so was me. I found that the way I spent my days held no value, gained no recognition, had no audience but me. I had no idea how well or badly I was doing: no feedback, no benchmark, no target but the indeterminate one of 'giving them the best'. Chris used to ring up to say: 'I'll be working late at the office, dear.' (Or forget to ring up, and therefore come home even later, in the hope that I'd be asleep and he could save himself a rollicking.) I would lovingly prepare a superb dinner, which was dry and crinkled by the time Chris got home and couldn't face it anyway, having spent a week on hotel fare. I looked forward to the evening for an account of Real Life in the Big World outside the sitting-room; and became resentful and disappointed when he crashed out, pole-axed, in front of the television.

Meanwhile, Chris says: 'You didn't appreciate how vulnerable I was. I didn't feel in control. I had three dependents on a low income, so we were financially stretched. It was tough. Moving between the two worlds was difficult. There was so much going on at work, but it wasn't relaxing at home. It was a minefield. You were always trying to jusify what you'd done, and I had to make sure I said the right things about dinner, and remember to notice when you'd cleaned the house. The kids impacted very little on my life. What I remember best is the horror of the nappy bucket. I always felt I wanted to do my share, but I probably didn't. There was always a lot of stuff around, toys to clear up, stacks of washing-up, as though you were waiting for me to come home and sort it out. I couldn't just sit down. There was no joy in it. So much seemed to be expected of me. And you weren't a companion any more.'

In a follow-up to the Rapoports' research, Suzan Lewis found in 1991 that most married or cohabiting women in the UK are employed; but most take a break from full-time employment after having children. A major reason why they do is the belief, strongly held in Britain, that young children require full-time mothers. It's no longer seen precisely as a crime for mothers to work, but Lewis quotes interesting statistics which suggest that traditional attitudes still hold sway: in contrast to the 78 per cent of women questioned in the Sixties who thought that mothers shouldn't work, only 45 per cent still thought so in a 1988 survey – but even then a further 29 per cent thought mothers should only work if they needed the money. Britain seems more prescriptive than other countries about the exclusive role of its mothers, and women bear the brunt of this.

Despite this emphasis on caring for the next generation, women who plump for home-making still risk being completely discounted as 'just housewives', particularly in comparison to the heights being achieved by some women in the workplace – because the criteria of measurement are all to do with status in the Big World. It's harder now to choose to stay at home, when you're deafened by exhortations to get on and fulfil your potential. Research quoted by Lewis suggests that mothers who intend to return to work, but don't, are under much more stress a year later than mothers who do return, and the husbands of mothers who are not employed are also more stressed than fathers with working spouses. Juggling job and home may be difficult, but it's less stressful than being a full-time mother who is used to working outside the home – or, indeed, her other half.

Some women feel as frustrated in full-time motherhood as I did, but decide to stick with it. If the woman doesn't go back to work, or takes some years out to bring up the children, the psychological cost may be enormous. One woman's experiences were particularly poignant because she and her husband had started their careers in parallel. 'When we met we were both training for our profession. I won all the prizes. Then we had to make a decision about whose career to follow, and it had to be Mark's, because he was so ambitious, so I compensated by taking jobs I could get which would fit his. They didn't fit me, but that couldn't be helped. Then we had two children, so I became a full-time Mum to make a good job of bringing them up. Now he owns his own company, and I am just starting to work part-time again. I know what it means to mourn – I did, for a long time, after my brother died. And now I'm grieving for my lost career.'

Why not stay-at-home fathers? Men have to give reasons, now that the Breadwinner and his Wife Syndrome is not axiomatic. I've lost count of the times men have quoted juvenile crime statistics as a reason why women should not be at work. Their message is still that care of the next generation is more glorious than personal fulfilment, and women are, by history and tradition, the obvious candidates to provide it. (New Men with their fingers crossed.) Other arguments for not reversing roles are economic. One insurance salesman was proud of his wife's part-time job as a speech therapist. I asked him why she worked at all. 'For quality of life, to keep our standards up,' he replied. I asked him why she didn't work full-time. 'Because somebody has to look after the children, and I can earn more than she can. She would like to work full-time, and I wouldn't mind working shorter hours, but we couldn't keep the quality we have now if we reversed roles.' It's too true that pioneers in role reversal may have to settle for less in consumer terms. Women do tend to earn less than men. When hourly rates are compared, women in the UK average 78 per cent of the men's rate. It will take positive action to balance that asymmetry. A report by the Equal Opportunities Commission in September 1992 stated that existing laws are not having an impact on pay rates for women. Evidence from other countries shows that, in addition to market forces, custom, practice, social values and organisational systems have a part to play in determining pay levels.

Chris says now: 'Underlying all the arguments is the assumption that looking after small kids is a pain in the butt. If it's a pain in the butt, it ought to be shared; if it isn't, then there's value in it, so you ought to get some. You start from the 'given' that men don't relate to small kids, and at the same time women exercise an air of proprietorship over them, as though they're the only people who can. But maybe having to do it would teach men to put somebody else first, and be aware of needs which aren't articulately expressed. It would switch us on to other people.' Indeed, there are signs of change. Latest research on two-career couples suggests that many men are beginning to be very much concerned about juggling family and career. There are men who accommodate their career to their family or spouse's needs. One assessment consultant is encouraged by the number of men who are putting constraints on their mobility and chances of promotion in order to protect their children's ability to follow the school curriculum, now that it depends so much on continuous course-work. Many men now spend significant amounts of time on childcare, although not as much as women. It looks as though their definition of their parental contribution is moving, from bringing home the wherewithal to Being There. Some have tried, but couldn't hack it. 'I was going to stay at home and look after the kids,' said a computer engineer. 'I lasted a month. I don't know how women do it.' Yes, indeed. One psychologist coped by thinking of it all in organisational terms. 'I managed the squadron while I was in the Fleet Air Arm; when I left the Navy I spent time managing the kids.' Such role reversals are new, under-developed and far from universally accepted. In some cases men are being forced into considering them because of losing their jobs; but often it's as a direct result of the options that women are taking up.


**Full-time working father / part-time working mother.** Two-and-a-half years of being a full-time housewife and mother were enough for me. The timing seemed ideal when we bought a run-down market garden. We faced all the demands of a strugglng new business, including a not inconsiderable overdraft. So I went back to work – part-time. I looked after the boys all day, and did the book-keeping for the business all night. If the VAT man came to inspect us, I fitted him in between school runs.

My part-time job was under my control, although it didn't feel like it at the time. Other women are much more at the mercy of employers. Part-time work fits in with family commitments, which is why 90 per cent of part-time workers are women. But it offers reduced money, challenge, prospects and status. Women's financial contribution to the domestic exchequer is therefore negligible, and they compensate by assuming even more of the responsibility for chores and service at home. Which reduces their opportunities for taking better-paid full-time work, thus neatly completing the vicious circle.

It may be a joint decision to have children, but it's still seen as the woman's job to look after them. If a woman does return to work, it's perceived as her own free choice, even when the family needs the money. If the choice is hers, then, of course, she is accountable for making it work – so all the organisation and timetabling remains her responsibility. 'Who are the friends of the working mother?' I asked a solicitor. 'I don't know about friends,' she replied, 'but school is the enemy. They cancel Sports Day when you've freed it up so you can be there, and reschedule it without notice for the day when you've got ten appointments.'

For my part, whatever I was doing, I felt I should be doing something else. It was like being a single parent: Chris was never there. He says: 'I saw myself as working incredibly hard and being the driving force. My focus was very much outside the family. I expected meals to be cooked and ready when I wanted them, and the house to be tidy. I wanted the freedom to be something different from what you wanted me to be. You resented the time I spent on the business and its encroachment on home and family. All I wanted from you was service; if you tried to muscle in on decision-making, it felt like an invasion. In one sense, the only way you can deal with the responsibility of being a father is to ignore it. What gives you the drive to go out and make a living is to be insensitive. It's hard on the one hand to have sufficient drive to make it in the Real World, and on the other to come home and be a warm family person. For the first time I was experiencing the pleasures, frustrations and hurt of combat in the Real World. When I came home I wanted comfort, sex, slippers and some food. I was completely unaware of your needs – and you sure as hell didn't appreciate mine.'

**Single working mother and week-end father.** The next main event was divorce. Patterns are now starting to change, but it's still nearly always the woman who has care and control of children after separation, as I did. I really was a single parent now. All my responsibilities constantly clashed. I maintained three part-time jobs – administering the business, and teaching French and German at a comprehensive by day and adult education classes in the evenings. For a while I couldn't even keep one of my classes in order at school. I was lonely. I was afraid I would not be able to support the boys, or give them enough time. I tried the breadwinner's excuse for failure to provide 'quality time': survival comes first, and *somebody* has to be out earning the living. I did not convince myself. Under such conditions the constant threat is fatigue and overload. Given all this, you can suffer, you can rationalise, or you can turn into Superwoman. Me, I rationalised, and paid in bad dreams. I mugged up theories about being a Good Enough Mother, and how to avoid Smother Love; I didn't take the kids out on the spree, but let them see what the Real World was like by taking them to the office and making them hang around while I did what people do in offices; I taught them to shop and cook and clean so that they would be infinitely more autonomous than I was when I left home; I tried to treat the family as a team, so that each could contribute according to capacity and withdraw according to need. But I still wondered whether in years to come my sons would remember me best as a slave-driver, or a Mum there in body but not in spirit.

Chris says: 'I hated having nobody to go home to. That was the key at that time: to be able to go home to a kindred spirit who didn't put pressures on you. The boys became more important, because I realised I might lose them, and how much I had missed. They were old enough for me to do things with them; I could participate in their achievements in the outside world; they became real outside the limits of the house.'

Reality to Chris was outside the domestic circle. Until we split up, reality to me was inside it, because of the boys. 'Divorce was a complete catalyst for you,' Chris says. 'It changed your perception of the status of work in the whole context of life.' True enough – and for him it was the idea of parenthood which changed. Each of us had failed to make the other understand the significance of the world where we had been specialists. It was as much a philosophical challenge to recognise the importance of the world we weren't familiar with, as it was a practical problem to take part in it. For each of us, it took a major crisis to unlock our perceptions of the new world we were forced to break into, and to revise the priorities which governed our actions.

**Jobless man, employed woman.** The next significant combination, after we'd started living together again, was when we'd sold our company. I re-trained, and Chris found himself without the business with which he'd identified himself over the previous eight years. Like me, he wanted to strike out in a new direction, but found he was too old at thirty-eight. At every turn he met rejection. At the same age, even with my zigzag work record, I looked a more sensible proposition. His history looked odd for a man. Mine looked typical for a woman. In some ways, you're more acceptable starting again in mid-life if you're female. Older men with a young man's drive to do something new and challenging may find they're seen as unemployable – too much authority, not enough specialist skill. I found an employer with the guts to take an untried package with limitations: school holidays off, reduced salary. He rubbed his hands. 'I know you'll give me 120 per cent anyway,' he purred. And so, indeed, it came to pass. Long hours, fax at home, writing reports on the boundary at the under-fifteen county cricket matches until it was time for me and the other Mums to prepare the tea.

I became the main breadwinner. The world was wide open,

terrifying, stimulating and exhausting. Suddenly it was me forgetting to ring in to say I'd be home late, and collapsing into a stupor when I arrived. I fell quite naturally into all the habits of superficial communication I'd deplored so bitterly when I'd been on the receiving end. It became unrewardingly effortful to repackage external excitements into the pinhead proportions that suited the supper-table. The boys were at school, and Chris didn't know how to validate his existence beyond doing exactly what I'd done as a housewife: listing all the chores he had completed during the day and waiting for brownie points. 'I felt guilty about stepping outside the flat, because everyone would see I wasn't working. I invested significance in everything: the washing-up, the coffee-breaks. I felt guilty if I took more than an hour for lunch. I kidded myself it mattered. You coming home was an Event, and I built the evening around it. I'd never realised what an impact it could have. When you were late it was as if you were nonchalantly playing with my time. When you asked about my day I saw it as condescending. I resented being dependent on you for money. You seemed to know where you were going, and I didn't. I felt very inadequate. It's different for a woman: there's an unwritten contract that a woman has kids and the man supports them all, but if you haven't got kids at home you don't have any right to be supported.' I was proud to have the chance of being the Breadwinner, but I couldn't say so because it undermined him. I felt cheated, he felt lost. He no longer had a marker in the Big World to tell him who or what he was, but he couldn't retreat into the Small World as women can, because there men are the outsiders, and he didn't have small children as an excuse.

Even for the short period when Chris didn't contribute money to the household, he could hardly bear it. He came to terms with it by treating my income as a quid pro quo for the years in which he supported me and the babies, as though he'd built up a credit from which it was now all right to withdraw. I didn't see that as part of the same deal at all. I felt he'd already had his return on that investment: I'd paid in kind, as chief cook and bottlewasher for all those years. He was defensive and I was aggrieved. We moved very delicately; it was easy to put a foot wrong, and set off agonies of resentment either way.

The expectation of life as a Breadwinner climbing up a ladder brings a combination of psychological security and obligation for many men. They can experience a foretaste of hell if recession or organisational change take their ladder away. A place on the ladder is how they measure themselves, and without it they have no identity. Not to be safely on a rung with another one up ahead makes you a nowhere man.

Women who achieve more than their partners, or who earn more, contradict the historical pattern. This can create a relationship perceived as unbalanced, threatening and stressful, even if part of the initial attraction for the man was the woman's competence and strength. Some women sacrifice hopes of promotion for an undamaged marriage. Others take the promotions and face (or manufacture) problems at home. I heard about a couple in late middle age: the man had just been made redundant, and the woman was making great strides in her career. 'She's not above turning the knife in the wound,' said my informant. It's equally threatening to some women if men take over the domestic role. I feel inadequate when Chris cleans the loo. It's not a man's job, is it?

**Joint breadwinners.** After a year or so of trying to break new ground, Chris decided that the only way to achieve the satisfaction and autonomy he needed was to go into business again on his own account. So he established his own company, built up a team and a network, and invested in training. Now both of us work all hours, and for days at a time neither of us cleans the loo and we live on baked beans. We manage with difficulty to maintain our record of at least one of us always being there on important occasions for the boys. Their holidays would be a nightmare for us all if they weren't so independent and thoughtful. I've lost not only the capacity, but the desire to be the warm embodiment of home. Home is now more of a place where four individuals facilitate one another's activities. I've also lost my strong need to have a Breadwinner to cling to, but I'm still not quite reconciled to *being* one. Chris says: 'Life's easier now, because the nature and the scale of our mutual dependency have changed. We expect a lot less from each other – and probably get more.'

**How was it for you?** Life has not been what either of us expected. After what looks, in retrospect, like a series of disastrous experiments between ourselves under the impact of work and parenthood, we wish we had known earlier what we know now. We know that the unbalanced expectations and needs of women and men can make any action problematical; clearcut individual decisions may hit reefs when the two halves of a couple try to manoeuvre their joint existence; children's requirements vary substantially over time, and arrangements which suit toddlers won't do for adolescents. Any of the combinations we've experienced ought to have worked, if only we had appreciated the psychological legacies, and understood and agreed the contracts, as well as more-or-less competently fixing practical emergencies as they arose.

The solid nature of men's expectation as they follow in their father's footsteps certainly creates its own difficulties. The ladder may look awfully steep, and men may be prepared these days to open up a bit and admit weaknesses their Dads might have thought twice about revealing. 'I often feel completely out of my depth,' said a middle manager in an oil company. They may come to loathe the ladder. I have met several male managers in the throes of existential angst. 'Who am I? What's it all for? Is this all life is? How can I get off this treadmill?' Men can no longer rely on either a job for life, or a woman who will serenely consent to be a Breadwinner's Wife. It's usually been women who have shifted from role to role, and they know how hard it is to keep matching the role with the appropriate behaviour. Now it's becoming likelier that men will have to do likewise. It's much more of a novelty, but one which they will have to come to terms with. Women and men achieve comparable results at college, and express equal commitment to work and to family. But men still don't, on the whole, have to regard work and family as trade-offs – and women do. Men may be forced to re-evaluate such trade-offs. Many men are very complimentary about the balance women bring to their lives; others see the account of the complexities of juggling as a series of alibis for getting nothing right, or futile whingeing against the inevitable. Men can't have it all any more then women can, but there are more things in heaven and earth than some of them think to look for. Men's challenge is to question whether accepted goals are enough, and to find out if they're missing something good before the opportunity slides by, or crisis hits and they find themselves bereft of resources.

It has really only been in the last couple of generations that women have been able to express goals their mothers didn't have. Thirty years ago few women found it natural to voice long-term career aims, and if they did they were modest. Women have had two generations of being in the workplace in increasing numbers, and one generation of Equal Opportunities. Even my generation has been far from universally involved in full-time careers. Women's tradition in attempting the climb is much shorter and more precarious than men's. Two generations of spotty infiltration are not enough to shake off the established sense that what men aim to do is the norm. The result is that any aims expressed by women – work full-time, work part-time, stay at home and bring up a family – can be characterized as ever so slightly unnatural. Women's achievements should be reassessed in positive terms: what they have actually done is to deploy as much flexibility as they can find, and men should take such flexibility as a model. Women can't *have* it all, but they shouldn't try to *do* it all, either, or the price can be too steep. From the inside it feels like not giving quite enough to any of it, and seeking reassurance that it will at least do. It would be an advance not to hear women in the twenty-first century talking like this Royal Mail manager: 'I suffer the guilt of the world when I haven't cleaned the house, fed the kids, done a full day's work and ravished the old man.'

## Organisations and the crossover

Looking at the workplace, you could be forgiven for thinking that most employers were stuck in a timewarp. It's as though none of the immense social changes we have seen in the last thirty years has impacted on life in what Chris insists on calling the Real World, as if the Small World weren't just as real. However, employers still assume the world is full of married men. Work is still largely structured for Breadwinners who have wives, and anyone who doesn't suit that template is a misfit.

**Women's work.** There's one exception to that, and that's the area of women's work. According to the traditionalists, the role of a real woman is to support; of a real man, to act. If the job they do has an equivalent profile, then at least one problem is resolved for both of them: the job is 'gender-appropriate', and it fits. It's all right for men to be firemen and Managing Directors. And so women can be nurses and secretaries, as though their real strength were to fulfil wife-Mum-and-housekeeper roles: faithful lieutenants, servicing the executives, and filling in gaps between the real actions that make life interesting and useful.

Women are still largely in service, support and people-orientated jobs: footwear and clothing, medical and health, personal services (including cleaning and hairdressing), selling, administrative and clerical, and catering. A similar share-out is found within functions inside organisations. Women are perceived as suited to staff rather than line positions, where they can use their interpersonal and organising skills; so they end up in personnel and administration rather than operations. Within functions which are not so obviously appropriate for women, some women choose, and some feel forced, to focus on the least 'masculine' aspect of the job. Many top flight female journalists write about fashion and women's issues, not politics or sport. Female lawyers and police officers often specialise in children and family problems, not crime and fraud. After all these years, the assumption still exists that there are such things as women's work and men's work.

Women are often very happy with a gender-appropriate support role. This may be because the job consists of things they actually enjoy doing and are good at; because they like to please and be of service; because they place higher value on caring than competing; because they lack confidence to take a risk and do something different, and there aren't enough role-models to inspire them; or because they don't like what happens to women in unusual areas when things go wrong. Mrs Thatcher became caricatured as a man. Senior women in sex discrimination cases are sometimes gratui- tously smeared as good-time girls. Kate Adie was forced to leave Libya when she was reporting on the war there for the BBC, because her pressure on the Government became characterized by Libya's Information Ministry as the actions of a nag and a virago: 'She never hesitates in insulting and scolding our representatives as if they are her own slaves.'

The notion that there are women who don't do women's work rings alarm bells. If you're not a man, a mother, a tart or an angel, what on earth are you? 'Women don't seem safe in an atypical role,' said the owner of a small business. 'Men are unsafe in a predictable way: they're after your throat!' Some men think that women only choose an unusual role to make a political statement, not because they simply like the job. A site manager talked about a female civil engineer who had difficulties with the construction workers on the site, and one day, he says, ran off in tears. 'She only took the job because she was a feminist,' he says, dismissively. The key issue is acceptance for what you are, but the limelight shines on apparent misfits, or reduces them to safe levels. A letter to the *Sunday Times* on 19 April 1992, after the General Election, asked: 'Is Michael Portillo attractive? Married? What does his wife do? Does he do the cooking at home? Or are these facts only important if the minister in question is a woman? Your profiles of Bottomley, Shepard and Portillo in mentioning the appearances and marital status of the women, but not of the man, will only help to perpetuate the gender stereotypes which are largely responsible for the 1:10 male/female ratio in the new Cabinet. If women are ever to achieve equality in the professions, they must stop being regarded as wives and mothers first.'

It would be a sign of complacency to assume that women are performing support roles solely because they want to, and don't have the capacity to operate elsewhere. Women may be choosing not to risk sex-role conflict in themselves or prejudice in others – both of which may be more painful than they're worth.

Men are generally happier when women are in 'suitable' jobs.

'Women are wonderful,' said the Rector of a rural benefice, 'because they are so good at supporting men.' There's hardly a man who won't tell you: 'Women are great organisers.' A manager in the oil industry said: 'Women are so good at people, it's a shame to waste their capacities on operations.' Flattery about one source of excellence is used to cut people out of potential for others. 'Women should play to their strengths.' Perhaps it's a coincidence that many of women's strengths as perceived by men seem to be in backroom, subordinate, non-executive, gluing, non-competitive roles. The Chairman of one large organisation is proud of his mainly female workforce, spread over all levels. He says: 'One of the good things about working with women is that they are not after my job.'

'Women's work' is devalued. Secretaries used to be men, and the job had status. When typewriters came in, and nimble-fingered women began to operate them, both pay and status shrank. Men doing 'women's work' are often promoted quickly, and they provoke interesting reactions. A male secretary reported in the *Independent* of 26 August 1992 that he often met, from the men who dealt with him, patronising underestimation of his intelligence; and from the women, unofficial promotion. They described him as 'a consultant'.

Some research suggests that 'women's work' is less satisfying. Men and women employed in occupations where the majority of workers are men have higher work satisfaction than those in women-dominated occupations, even when factors such as education record, level of supervision, and earnings are balanced out. Men's work is seen as more prestigious and lucrative; women's as lacking in authority and autonomy. Indeed, women's work does tend to pay less. On average, in 1971, a year after the Equal Pay Act, women were earning 65 per cent of men's salaries. By 1976 it had increased to 75 per cent, and has remained at about that level ever since. Women earn less than men, even when they are in comparable jobs. There's a spiral of devaluation, firstly of the jobs that women do, and secondly of women in any job.

It's very wasteful for the organisation, and limiting for individuals of both sexes, if artificial boundaries stop them applying for other jobs they would enjoy and do well. Being superb at organising things and handling people is a bonus for the holder of any job; so confining women to personnel is shortsighted. At the same time, woolly-minded definitions of certain roles or occupations as 'women's work' also make them seem less attractive or welcoming to men, so that organisations lose out on the additional value men might bring to them. Women's flexibility between roles can turn into a weakness, so that they end up solely in the ones men are not so good at. These then become by definition women's work and less valuable overall to the organisation, so that there is no incentive for men to be good at them, which increases the divide between men's and women's work. Organisations miss out on individuality, balance and a new approach.

**Priority, visibility, commitment.** Unwritten criteria for a credible day's work are very inflexible. People have to be single-minded, willing to put in all the hours that God sends, and to jump at the Company's behest. It's not enough to produce value: you also have to be seen to be doing it. The emphasis is often on quantity rather than quality, input rather than output: perhaps a masculine orientation, where it's necessary to be *seen* to be active. Businesses benefit by more interesting, more relaxed people with deeper motivations and broader perspectives of what life can offer. And yet organisations don't encourage them. A male Personnel Director: 'Successful people work long hours, attend conferences away, don't keep an eye on the clock, are at the company's disposal, body, heart and soul. Women go home to their families. Men don't respect that. The choice is to resist company culture – the late nights, the early mornings, the extra night at the hotel for that important meeting'. Resisting the culture is not a respectable standpoint if it's viewed in terms of letting down the company. Sometimes such constraints become a sort of commitment test. It's as though the company were asking: how much will you sacrifice to keep this job and make something of it? If it's less than everything else, you're not the man we thought you were. And, sure enough, you probably aren't.

Visibility is very important. 'It stands to reason that you can't be a proper manager if you're only around from 9 till 3 four days a week.' Why on earth not? Many managers are around far less than that, with all their meetings and presentations. Some of the best managers delegate like maniacs, and trust their staff enough to risk being unreachable a lot of the time. The sense of a manager's contribution is very much in the eye of the beholder: women's absence is attributed to non-work demands (shopping for the family); that of men is attributed to other working duties (extended meeting). A man saying he'll be in late because his car is playing up (an accident) is more acceptable than a woman taking time off because a child is sick (a competing priority).

However, many women are already testing how amenable organisations are to change. Anna Turnbull-Walker, a solicitor and *She* magazine's 'Working Mother of the Year' in 1991, instigated changes which seem obvious to anyone who has ever been a 'working mother' but which she had to fight for, tooth and nail: breakfast meetings instead of the ones which made her miss the children's bedtime, half-days working at home. Senior women in the Royal Mail are asking to perform a four-day week, or to work from home unless commitments demand their presence elsewhere; and the answer they are starting to receive is 'Yes, provided you meet your objectives'. Most often these are women who are confident they have proved their worth during their younger, 'workaholic' phase, and already have the faith and trust of the organisation they work for. Eventually, perhaps, it will be possible to go straight into such an arrangement, without having to prove commitment by overwork first. Job shares have been on the agenda for years, at least in the public sector, but have never achieved popularity generally, although isolated cases have proved extremely successful. Some organisations do respond, albeit passively, to requests from people to operate outside the habitual routine. What's generally missing is proactive encouragement within organisations for men and women to discuss what options exist for integrating all aspects of life, and how these options can be transformed into practical activity. We need a change of mindset here. Rather than assuming that a smaller than 100 per cent commitment to their job diminishes a worker's credibility, we should believe that total credibility demands a much wider commitment to all areas of life.

**Certainty and stability vs uncertainty and expense.** At work women face a further barrage of negative perceptions. If they have children they're potentially unreliable. If they haven't, depending on their age, they've either got it all before them – or there's something wrong with them. If a woman is good at her job, the assumption is often that she has achieved this at the cost of failing elsewhere. A little experiment: ask people to guess the marital status of a successful woman at work, and they are more likely than not to guess she's separated, divorced, or never married. And the perception is based on reality. In a survey on management attitudes to women carried out among its members by the British Institute of Management in 1992, 92 per cent of the male respondents were married or living with a partner, and 68 per cent of the women. 83 per cent of the men had children, and 41 per cent of the women. One of the principal strategies adopted by many women who want careers is to opt out of children, certainly, and often long-term relationships as well. This gives them just the one focus for their lives, and enables them to avoid the pressure of guilt. The current birth-rate in the UK is 1.6 children per woman – one of the lowest in Europe. It's much less easy to opt out of elderly parents, and responsibilities here will create more and more dilemmas as the population ages.

If a woman lives alone, the speculation can go as far as her sexual proclivities. One woman who won a sexual discrimination case against her employer amid avid media coverage felt obliged publicly to repudiate oblique Press conjecture that she was a lesbian. Somehow a woman's competence at work suggests that her home role will be lonely, atypical, or failed. There is no comparative spotlight on a competent man.

A young manager encapsulated the feeling that men are the only secure option: 'There is nothing in life a man cannot prepare himself for.' Women are often perceived to be asking organisations to commit themselves to a route of uncertainty and expense. Or, as a retail manager put it: 'We don't trust women or their motives.' A man with a wife is perceived as being stable because of the support he *gets* at home; a woman with a husband is perceived as being unstable, because of the support she *gives* at home.

**Pregnant pause.** We do have to deal with the fact that 'working women' give birth. A service station manager claimed afterwards to have been joking when he stated that he only employed persons without ovaries. Will she, won't she launch into maternity? If she does, will she come back – or will she say she's going to, and then not do it?

Pregnancy causes great inconvenience for organisations. Maternity rules about leave and pay can be a huge burden, particularly in smaller businesses. Employers can feel inclined to avoid any risk. According to Susan McRae, author of a Policy Studies Institute report into working mothers, the majority of employers accept maternity as part of business life. Only one per cent of women in her survey lost their jobs as a result of being pregnant. However, as she points out, that still adds up to a lot of women – and there may be more losing their jobs, under the guise of voluntary redundancy and job elimination, as a result of the reorganisations caused by recession. Sometimes jobs are redefined with such stringent demands that it is impossible for anyone with dependents to fulfil them. Effectively, this excludes women.

In old-fashioned professions pregnancy can cause a distinct flutter in the dovecotes. The Bar doesn't have clearcut maternity policies. Barristers' Chambers have a code of conduct, as among gentlemen. 'As long as we *are* fair – and we are – we don't need to lay down specific rules.' (Men's eternal cry to women – 'Trust me!') However, not labelling things keeps them woolly. Understandings may not be shared in the cold light of day. Unless things are cut and dried it's all too easy to hide behind a gentleman's agreement, and never be brought to account. Every step of the way forward becomes another personal hazard to be renegotiated; and of course the 'guidelines' are unspoken and variable. One barrister wanted her rent waived while she was away producing her family. After considerable debate she obtained a reduction by using the argument that it was a long-term economy: she was expecting twins and would be asking only once.

Cases like the Preisler vs Buggins furore in 1991 spotlight the pregnancy issue, but don't help to resolve it. Preisler had a £150,000 a year job in the City. She became pregnant, lost her job, and took Buggins, her boss, to a tribunal claiming discrimination and constructive dismissal. She got a month's salary in compensation for constructive dismissal, but the discrimination case was thrown out. The case was noteworthy because both protagonists were women. At the time a manager in the City was quoted as saying: 'There is a violent conflict between the rights of the customer and the whimsical desires of some of these women. They want twentieth-century rights and nineteenth-century privileges . . . Because of the legislation, I would not employ a woman. Women have made themselves unemployable. They have scored an own goal.' Tribunals exist for the examination of such issues, but women mostly do not take legal action, for fear of spoiling their own future and creating a damaging precedent for others. The *spirit* of the maternity laws is intended to protect women from abuse by their employers; often the *letter* of the law is interpreted by employers as exposing them to abuse by mothers. The state imposes laws on organisations to ensure that pregnant women get a fair deal – and although it has an interest in future generations it doesn't back up law by funding. The cost of maternity is borne by organisations and individuals. Women, however, get the blame.

There's the possibility that pregnancy at work has a psychological effect, too. These days more women work while they are pregnant, and more during the last few months of pregnancy. There is little research on the effect of women's pregnancy on work. One laboratory study – with all the constraints and limitations that implies – compared the interactions of working people with two female 'managers': one pregnant, one not. Afterwards, those who had taken part said they were less happy about their interview with the pregnant manager, and recounted more negative impressions of her. Reactions included discomfort, confusion and hostility, in both men and women. They felt she was less fair in her dealings with subordinates, although they found no difference in her effectiveness or communication skills. It's possible that the pregnant manager did not live up to the expectation that she would behave in a soft, vulnerable, non-aggressive way – which is how people expect pregnant women to behave.

The (male) manager of an insurance company said to me: 'It's fine for women to take an equal position at work, and I understand about the difficulties of having small children – I've two of my own

– but things to do with the family, and what happens outside office hours, should be invisible. They don't belong at work. If you're at work that's all you should take account of.' And, of course, pregnant women *literally* carry the results of outside activity into the workplace, and remind their colleagues about sex and family and the role of mothers. It's not possible totally to be confined to the needs of the relevant business present when somebody is sitting there carrying an irrelevant non-business future inside them. Dealing with pregnancy is one more thing which does not appear on male organisational agendas.

After pregnancy comes child-care. It costs money and generates hassle to set up job-share schemes and run creches, and many organisations decide that such facilities are not cost-effective. They are seen as accommodating *women's* needs, not family needs or society's needs. An assumption rife in most organisations is that fathers of young children are not rethinking their ideas. Women do get at least some support in moving into masculine realms, but New Men get a rough deal. One top man in an international company was scathing about a Managing Director he knew. 'He had an awful work ethic. Do you know he used to go home early on Fridays because his children were due back from school?' Many criteria are applied to women which could equally benefit men. Is it really only women who can operate effectively within non-standard working hours? One Director felt he had taken a very enlightened step. 'We've learned to live with maternity. I've got a woman who's just been on maternity leave. She's brilliant. I set her up with a three-day working week, and told her she could have more days off if she wanted.' I asked if he would consider doing this for a woman who was not brilliant, but only average. 'Average? Yes, I think I would. It's the proper thing to do.' And for a man? 'A man. No, I have an instinctive reaction against men asking for a three-day week.' Why? 'It's not something you expect of a man. It wouldn't seem appropriate.' There are moves in the right direction. The Confederation of British Industry revealed in January 1993 a dramatic increase in paternity leave, from 32 per cent of the companies surveyed in 1987 to 76 per cent in 1992. However, for over half of the companies paternity leave was discretionary, and for most it was two or three days only. Time off was more likely to be given for Territorial Army training.

If younger men and their partners come to more equal divisions of contribution at home and at work, organisations which still operate as though all children are fatherless and all men are childless risk being cut off from the safety of their old, traditional resource. Who knows how far things may go? My father wouldn't push me in my pram. My partner pushed his sons *and* changed their nappies. Will there come a moment when men clamour for creches? There's very little encouragement for them to reassess their family commitments without penalty at present. One company proudly announced the introduction of a workplace creche as part of its drive to get more women on board. The day it opened, many Dads who already worked for the company brought along their children, thus releasing their wives to go and work somewhere else. The company shut the creche.

**Complacency.** Organisational roles are defined by functional job descriptions. But the pressure of stereotypes, prejudices and expectations leads to tension and waste. Most organisations concentrate on the wrong thing: the cost of making everybody fit into the old ways of doing things. How does the thinking go?

- Women as a sex are particularly suited to certain functions, and those functions are reflected in specific roles at work.
- Life outside the organisation is separate and negligible. If the job isn't top priority for employees, they have disqualified themselves as serious contributors. Value is proved by quantity of input; commitment is confirmed by visibility.
- Men are more programmable. They represent certainty and stability. Women represent uncertainty and expense.

It's a startling summary which gives evidence not only of inflexible thinking but of complacency and shortsightedness. The impact of social and family changes, the ambitions of men and women, the changes in the nature of work itself, the fluctuations of the economy – all these influences can weaken gender boundaries and make a strategic rethink imperative for organisational decision-makers.

Decision-makers may underestimate the impact of the dialogue between the sexes as it continues into the home. Gender roles in families are undergoing changes, albeit slowly. There's a lot of ambiguity, which we should welcome as it begins to dissolve constraints. Psychologist John Archer quotes research into gender ambivalence among young people: 'Girls don't play football – but a lot do, now.' New generations of workers will be less hide-bound by tradition.

Younger generations of men at work create a new atmosphere. Responses by two airline pilots, son (aged forty) and father (recently retired), to questions about women at work, show the extent of the generation gap. Son thinks there is absolutely no reason to exclude women from being pilots, provided they do not expect special treatment. Father doesn't question their talent, but thinks they should set up their own all-female airlines, because otherwise they are snatching the bread from the mouths of the men. This is very much an older man's fear. As one male Detective-Constable put it: 'Younger chaps are more liberal and fairer. Older ones are very narrow-minded – they don't have much time for women.'

Women need and want to work, and are spot-lighting the difficulties of doing so. At the same time, the profile of the workplace is changing. Service industries are increasing, and manual work decreasing. This is a world where powerful biceps attract less of a premium than flexibility and interpersonal skills. The new opportunities are gender-neutral – but women have already put in a good deal of practice in the skills they require. Women have a history of *not* getting the best jobs, but they tend to get the new ones. In the ten years to 1992 more than nine of every ten new jobs created went to women. At the same time, in a recession, men are less fussy about definitions of 'women's work'. They take the jobs they can get. Many are also willing to lower their sights in terms of pay and progress, if the alternative is unemployment. On the other hand, the recession has also demonstrated that women executives tend to gain new jobs after redundancy more quickly than men, in an average of three months rather than six. The likely reason is that women, having had to prove themselves and work harder, have more impressive qualifications.

For many reasons, then, gender boundaries at work are in the process of change. There is enough ambivalence in people's think-ing about the place of women at work to suggest that stereotypes are beginning to crumble. However, organisations are not, on the whole, putting enough effort into creating the right environment.

The Rapoports' Utopia has not been reached. Both partners may be afflicted by overload and conflict from juggling multiple roles. The stress endured by men and women in dual-career families is damaging to their performance at work, and therefore policies which give them time to be parents could also enhance their work contribution. Women's preoccupation with home and family is at least as much a *result* as a *cause* of their frustration in the workplace. As Lewis point out in her review of the status of dual-career families, initiatives attract attention, but they only exist in a small minority of organisations. Often they are mainly aimed at women, but they should be a family issue. Many of us are in the throes of an identity crisis, in which the old stereotypes battle with new demands. Progress in co-operation at home is dependent on changes happening simultaneously in organisations.

There are straws in the wind, be they ever so tiny. Jerry Cope, Personnel Director of Royal Mail, says: 'Something is definitely happening out there. I think women have got a better sense of balance between work and home – for whatever reason – and I see many signs of men rebelling against the system. For the first time recently, when a conference was called for a Sunday evening start, a Director made his apologies and arrived on the Monday morning – and it was accepted. There's something going on in terms of people's willingness to devote 110 per cent of their time to work. And it has started because women have made the balance between home and work visibly important.'

He's right. Women are the missing link between the Big World and the Small. They are the catalysts and the trail-blazers. It's because women ask questions, about what they really want and what they can reasonably get, that men have to re-examine their own role. Women should carry on doing it. Everybody needs to ask: am I enjoying what I'm doing? What should I be doing? Are there more fulfilling ways to spend my time? How much of my time can I devote to my own interests, and how much should I spend on less self-focused activities? What does being a wife/

husband/mother/father/employee mean to me? Does it mean the same thing to my partner? After all, the issue is not just about how to get more women into the workplace, but how to get more men to enjoy being out of it. Why confine the definition of 'success' to the working world alone? It needs to be combined with broader elements than just achievement at work. How about: happy children? A respected and well-cared for population of elderly people? A life of memorable and pleasurable moments? Five good friends? A transformed definition of 'success' has huge implications for change. Change inevitably means pain and sacrifice, but there must also be reward. Identity crises are at the forefront of a process which will get worse before it gets better. The best negotiations, they say, are those where both parties come out feeling they've won. Too often, at present, the options available in earning a living and running a home make both men and women feel like losers.

# 6 Close Encounters

For most of us, work is not only an end in itself, but an excuse for meeting people – a relationship-sustaining medium *par excellence*. For some 240 working days a year we are not only permitted, but positively encouraged, to form close relationships with colleagues, customers and suppliers. This is considerably more than the waking hours that those of us with partners get to spend in their company.

What organisations call for – and all they admit to, usually – are relationships based on liking and friendship. What they actually get in a workplace populated by men and women is both of those, plus love and sex as well – and the boundaries between them can become very fuzzy indeed. Of all the relationships that can be formed between people at work, the ones between men and women probably offer some of the most fulfilling rewards and the most excruciating penalties.

Sex and love have always haunted the workplace. The difference in today's world is that the historical balance of power is shifting. Men no longer solely occupy the dominant roles, nor women solely the subservient ones. The shake-up of the Breadwinner and his Wife syndrome has redistributed economic power and responsibility. Proportions are changing: women are still in a minority in many areas, but the number is growing all the time, and increasing the chances that men and women will have to get on at work at an equal level. There's a moral dimension, too. Thirty years ago the choice for women was much closer to the old tradition of 'marriage or job'. Twenty years ago half the married women in Britain worked. In 1990, according to the General Household Survey, 71 per cent of married women were working, and 72 per cent of single women. Nowadays, as more women with partners (married or not) take up jobs, a workplace in which men and women rub shoulders offers easy alternatives to monogamy. In the light of all these changes, both women and men have to re-evaluate traditional patterns of romantic and sexual behaviour.

This chapter is about close relationships between men and women at work. It is largely, but not exclusively, about the influence of sex on a two-gender workplace; and largely, but not exclusively, about how and why things go wrong, and what should be done about it.

It's not as though close relationships of the organisational kind are exactly rare. Men and women are interacting at all temperatures all over the British workplace, because they can't help noticing the sexual as well as the gender difference. Women and men don't need permission to be interested in each other: it's what we were put here for. Of course there are degrees of interest. Some people are much more conscious than others of the potential for a sexual element in any situation. And, if it's there at all, attraction doesn't disappear because work imposes tasks we are paid for. Men and women together at work don't only mean business, and it's shortsighted to pretend they do.

Listen to your colleagues on the telephone. I always know the sex of the person mine are talking to, just from their tone of voice. Women and men enjoy the difference. Men are intrigued by women. 'I find women fascinating,' observed Alec Reed with enthusiasm. A thirty-four-year-old male Managing Director: 'Women are so much more interesting than men. You never hear anything new from men – they are utterly predictable.' A lyrical customer service manager: 'Women are warm, vulnerable, demanding, essential. They need to be tougher. They are provocative and sensual (some more than others!) They are also susceptible, and they can be irrational.' Men are of absorbing interest to women. A teacher: 'I love working with men. You can have a laugh. What would we do without them?' A personnel officer: 'They're pretty predictable – a sure short cut to the heart of even an intelligent man is to be the office siren.'

A very senior manager – a grandfather, incidentally – said

bluntly: 'It's great to have women around. They give the place a sexual boost. Of course, it wears off after a while, and I don't suppose the younger generation notice it so much, because they've been brought up in a more permissive era.' I checked with some much younger men whether they ever experienced a 'sexual boost' at work. Their answers were matter-of-fact. 'Well, of course.' 'All the time.' 'Surprised you ask.'

Enjoyment of the company of the opposite sex can lead into more intimate liaisons. A survey on office relationships commissioned by the Alfred Marks Bureau and published in December 1991 gathered 479 replies. Three out of ten respondents had experienced at least one relationship at work, and seven out of ten had observed relationships. They weren't all just office flings: over half those experienced or observed led to marriage or cohabitation. The Christmas party was one obvious place for a relationship to start, but the most popular beginning was making an advance during working hours. Relationships were mostly between colleagues of the same status. Most of those who were involved in close relation-ships, or who observed them, thought they did not affect work output. If there was any effect, more onlookers than participants thought it was a bad one. Half those involved thought senior people were neutral in attitude, but nearly half of the observers thought senior people were slightly disapproving. Most thought colleagues' attitudes were neutral.

Work may offer individuals ambiguous situations and temp-tations. If you have a motive in the first place, it's not difficult to find opportunity and means. There's working late. There are conferences in hotels, which are outside routine and where alcohol often plays a conspicuous part. Here's one woman's reaction: 'The place is full of beds and candlelight dinners and there are whole clusters of possibilities at the back of my mind, so I carefully choose words and actions which will subtly make it crystal-clear that this is business, because I can't actually state point-blank that everything else is off the menu. Sometimes it goes wrong and my professional warmth is mistaken for personal warmth. If I try to find out a bit more about a chap it's because he's an interesting person or I'm doing my job, not because I'm trying a come-on, but I see them wonder sometimes.' Here's another woman's point of view: 'If I like the idea I start by doing a bit of manoeuvring to see whether sex is on the agenda, but if it isn't I go straight into business. There'd be other areas we could discuss if we were both men or both women, but not with one of each.'

Women's magazines present personal relationships as an occupational hazard: proximity makes the heart grow fonder. They warn women, particularly 'returners' to the workplace after a period of home-making, to be wary of the heady delights of being themselves again – independent, nobody's wife, mother or daughter. They are cautioned against the allurement of an office affair, where all the constraints, the negotiation and the chores of home are absent. Some magazines carry a helpline number you can ring if you fall in love with a colleague or boss. The voices at the other end run through a couple of relevant case studies and reassure you that it happens all the time, and you should only start worrying if it affects your work.

Supposing an attachment is voluntary and reciprocated, yet still appears to be damaging work performance? Being at work can make the management of strong attraction awkward on both sides. Full-blown love affairs do indeed happen, and can bypass or mix up hierarchical lines of authority and accountability. Even being married to a colleague can potentially endanger the organisation, especially if one partner leaves it to work elsewhere. If a relationship (or its cessation) appears to jeopardise security or productivity, official notice may have to be taken. It's a complicated business, and it raises a multitude of ethical, social and legal issues. Romance and chemistry can't be tied down in organisational documentation: 'Thou shalt not fall in love with thy colleague or line manager, and if thou dost, thou shall keep it secret, and play it cool, and if thou canst not, thou shalt resign forthwith, on the grounds that thy behaviour is prejudicial to good company order.' But at least organisations need to establish a clear general policy for the decisions they take, so that they are based on evidence no weaker than would be accepted in any other personnel enquiry. Otherwise, the accusation of sexual discrimination may be levelled. If it can be demonstrated that confidential information is being passed on, or could be, or that the appraisal or expenses mechanisms are being abused by the parties to the relationship, then disciplinary procedures can be used. If the grounds for action are more nebulous – disruption at the workplace, for instance – then the resolution should be based on work criteria, not gender: for instance, the more junior of those involved will be moved to a job elsewhere. One industrial tribunal considered the case of an employee whose husband left the office where they had been working together to take a job with a rival. Her employers offered to maintain her salary, but downgrade her post, thus giving her more restricted access to confidential information. She refused, they fired her, and the tribunal upheld the decision, which was based on strictly work-based yardsticks. However, in early 1992 a Sales Manager was sacked for an affair with a married colleague, and she also took her case to an industrial tribunal. Her employer claimed that she had breached her contract by behaving in an unseemly manner; the chairman of the tribunal thought it was completely unreasonable to cite a discreet office affair as grounds for dismissal. According to the Equal Opportunities Commission, it's quite common for women to leave their job after an affair with a man. They don't normally fight the verdict, because that would entail admitting the affair publicly. If incidences of sexual discrimination are to be avoided, the assumption must not be made that it should always be the woman who will leave or be moved.

Male–female relationships are usually only given official notice if they endanger some aspect of the organisation. Generally, it may be embarrassing or threatening for employers to admit the power of sex, rampant, behind the photocopier, and to accept that at work people are still sexual beings. True, there are things about male–female relationships we just don't admit at work. Have I ever sat through a business meeting fizzing gently with lust? Well, yes, actually, but I know the rules, so I don't suppose anyone noticed. And, sure enough, it's nobody's business but mine. Keeping sex under wraps may also seem, at first glance, more politically correct. 'I treat people all the same,' say many well-meaning managers keen to reject any implication of sexual discrimination. What they do, however, is to throw the baby out with the bathwater. In seeking to deny discrimination, they also deny there is a difference. But the difference is not one that can be denied. As Alec Reed, Chairman of Reed Personnel, observed: 'Women shouldn't be cloned like men – the sexes are complementary.' A two-sex workplace needs to offer an environment in which people have access to help in solving two-sex problems, and in which individuals and groups are protected from abuse.

In October 1991 a British doctor won £150,000 damages for slander when the allegations of sexual harassment brought against him by his ex-colleague were thrown out. This award was three times as high as the previous British record. The case followed the long, complicated soap opera of the Judge Clarence Thomas sexual harassment case in the States earlier in the year, when television viewers saw the unfolding of a blow-by-blow account of every risqué comment and every suspect approach alleged to have been made by the judge; and it worried workers and employers in all corners of the globe. The British judge in the doctor's case told the jury the Clarence Thomas affair had resulted in 'our awareness of inter-gender relationships in the workplace being heightened and made more sensitive. Such relationships might never be the same again in the workplace, in offices, hospitals, doctors' surgeries, barristers' chambers – perhaps in the jury room and judges' corridors.'

Heightened and more sensitive our awareness may be; it also seems to be both limited and unofficial. *Gender*, like race and disability, is certainly an official item in equality initiatives, with the focus on policies, numerical targets, sexual discrimination, and how to avoid tribunals. *Women* are on some organisational agendas, with offers of assertiveness training, or leadership skills for women managers. But *inter-gender relationships*, including sexual harassment, often don't appear at all. A survey for the Alfred Marks Bureau in 1991 on sexual harassment in the office analysed 546 replies. Eight per cent of respondents knew of a formal written grievance procedure, 4 per cent of an informal unwritten procedure, 11 per cent said there was no procedure, and 77 per cent didn't know. Only 10 per cent didn't believe a procedure was necessary.

The Judge Clarence Thomas case caused many British managers to take fright. Was this the shape of things to come in the UK? There were two main areas for concern. Were there unknown victims who felt offended by certain words and behaviour? And were there people perpetrating distasteful acts, on whom a secret dossier was being amassed which could eventually cause trouble? At least in some organisations the unspoken did become spoken, and both areas of concern researched, sometimes less because of an interest in individuals' moral welfare than because of a perceived need for self-protection.

Some managers formally assembled their teams and investigated the issues. Often the evidence was inconclusive, but the discussion clarified a number of boundaries for people in the company. There were girlie calendars which gave silent offence – and large posters exhibiting masculine hunks which didn't. One manager's style was to put an arm round everybody he talked to, male or female. He suddenly realised that, because he was the boss, he might not be giving members of his team much of a chance to object, should they want to. So he called them all together, and asked them the question. He was reassured by the answer, but should probably have followed it up to check that the public nature of the meeting had not inspired a consensus result which some individuals disagreed with. In other companies managers simply sent informal recommendations along the grapevine: 'Chaps, whatever you normally do, stop doing it for three weeks, and see what happens. If the women complain because you're not doing it, start doing it again.' Nice thought, that one, but it didn't get any procedures set up. It was purely a short-term shock reaction.

Those organisations and their staff were lucky. Despite the absence of formal channels and procedures, they didn't have something nasty in the woodshed. Here is the story of a company which did.

## Thwarted passion

Judy Baker (not her real name) joined a small company as a young, ambitious clerk. It soon became clear to her that the job could be upgraded. There were skills she could learn, projects she could manage, responsibilities she could grow into. She worked long hours because she loved the job and the office camaraderie. Her manager, a married man of forty or so – let's call him Philip – was very complimentary about her work, both to her and to her colleagues, to the extent that it looked like favouritism and occasionally made trouble. One evening Philip tapped her backside as she leaned over the photocopier. Judy told him not to, but it was the first in a series of events and innuendos which ultimately made her leave her job.

Philip asked her to go out with him. She said no. She kept saying no. He said: 'I could ruin my life for you.' She tried explaining the effect he was having on her. He said: sorry, it was only office banter, he hadn't realised how she felt about it, he would cool it. He did cool it, but not for long.

He used to ring in to the branch office and insist on speaking to Judy. 'He would say sordid and disgusting things – like "What are you wearing? I bet you'd look wonderful in a black basque." He said to me in his office "I could quite easily rape you." I used to spend weekends with my fiancé, and Phlip said: "He only wants you for your body. I bet you visit him with your legs wide apart and your knickers round your ankles."' Many times Judy protested, and said she would report him to his boss. Philip retorted: 'Well, I'm the manager, and I've been here for 15 years. You've been here a month. You've been leading me on. My boss and I are old friends. Who do you think they will believe?' He said it was all her fault. She couldn't see how, but his repetition made her question the whole deal. Was there something she was doing, or not doing, which was making his actions inevitable? Was there something she herself should be doing, or not doing, which would restore a professional balance?

She found the situation bewildering. 'I didn't wear short skirts. I didn't wear open blouses. It's not the way I talk. There's nothing in my behaviour at all. So if it was me, it must have been something in my personality. Perhaps I am too friendly? But even then, I would have thought that even if I had been so friendly that he made the mistake at first, my reaction would have put him straight.'

Judy stuck it for three months, and then went to a solicitor to find out what her legal position was. After what felt to her like a cross-examination, the solicitor composed a letter to be sent to Philip. But he had left her with the impression that, even though he was supposed to be on her side, he did not fully believe her.

Either it was all in her imagination, or it was all her fault. So she couldn't bring herself to send the letter.

She hung on for a further three months. Then she took her itchy nettlerash, stomach cramps, insomnia, and lack of concentration to a doctor, who signed her off for 'nervous debility'. She took stock. She sent a letter of resignation to Philip, his boss, and the appropriate Director, with a copy of her sick note and the solicitor's letter. The Director came to see her, took her to neutral ground – a public wine bar – and discussed the issue in earshot of other customers. He said he would let her know the result of any disciplinary action which was taken, but never did.

Judy was nineteen then. She subsequently turned down two good jobs because the men in the office seemed so friendly that she suspected their motives. She took a post in an all-woman office, where she is very happy. Her first Christmas there, Simon, who works in the same building, asked her: 'Are you wearing suspenders and stockings, Judy?' She replied: 'Mind your own business!' She feels very guilty about this reply. 'It was an awfully rude thing to say, and not like me at all. I don't want to be rude. I don't want to offend people. Maybe I really am imagining things, and it is just office banter, and I should go along with it. Where does the banter stop and trouble start? I don't want to go through a similar episode again.'

Why did she stick it so long? 'I thought I could handle it. He kept saying it was just office banter, and I was used to that. I thought, as long as it's words and nothing else, I can cope with it. I thought I was strong enough, but I wasn't. I thought I could let it pass like water off a duck's back, but I was frightened to go with him to set up an exhibition unless someone else came too. I liked the job. I liked the other people in the office. They all knew about it, and tried to help. I thought: Why the hell should it be me that goes? I'm working hard, I'm not doing anything wrong, everybody is keen to work with me because I am good at my job. I thought: He's not going to win. This is a battle and I'm going to win it. I thought if I made a fuss I would have to face everybody, and they would all know how cheap and dirty it all was. All my male colleagues would think: Crumbs, we can't say anything to Judy any more, or she'll sue us. I hoped we would be able to resolve it. I liked his wife and the children – I didn't see why they should be made to suffer. I can take an awful lot. I suppose you learn to put others before yourself. I didn't want to disgrace my family.'

When in the end she resigned, she chose to let senior members of the organisation know why, partly on the advice of friends and colleagues, who urged her to save her successors. 'Could you live with it,' they said, 'knowing that he might be doing to somebody else what he did to you?' She wishes now she had done more. She thinks she was stupid, because she tried to go it alone, and did not call for help soon enough. She insists she did nothing wrong, but talks as though she had a guilty secret. If anything like it ever happened again, she says, 'I'd note down as much real evidence as possible, I'd find a *bloody* good female lawyer, and I'd take the whole thing a lot further, sooner.'

In that company there was no context for open discussion of any relationship issues at all. There was no policy or procedure in place. Any discussion could take no higher profile than general office gossip. Judy assumed that it was her personal duty as a professional woman to get on with her colleagues, and sort out difficulties entirely on her own. Her only recourse was through the line structure of the organisation, straight back to the offending manager. Philip implicated the whole company in his behaviour, and the company had no way of detecting what was happening. The result here was an employee lost to the company and sickened by it, a manager against whom serious allegations were made, an office full of distracted employees, and a clueless company taken by surprise and saved from public ignominy only by the sensitivity of the woman involved. It's when things go badly wrong that the organisation is shaken, unless it already has procedures in place during the good times. There may be no problem in your organisation – but can you be sure if the question is not raised?

Perhaps Philip was in love. He was entitled to the strong feelings he had, even towards someone who did not return them. What transformed feeling into harassment was his total disregard for the effect of his behaviour on Judy. Harassment is usually, though not always, this way round. Masculine power over women is role-appropriate, and the power role adds to the sexual role. The Alfred Marks surveys suggest that, on the whole, men are the main offenders and women the main victims; offenders tend to be senior staff, immediate boss or people at the same level; and the average age of offenders is about forty, and of victims about twenty-five.

In the well-regulated organisation employees need to be aware of a clear policy on harassment – ideally as part of the equal opportunities programme, and applicable to any form of harassment in which an individual is treated in a way which threatens their dignity. The Institute of Personnel Management's Statement on Harassment at Work maintains; 'Anyone who is perceived as being different, or who is in a minority, or who lacks organisational power, runs the risk of being harassed.' Managers should recognise that it is their responsibility to implement and monitor the policy, and it should be clear to every employee that they are responsible for their own behaviour. There must be opportunities for people who are being harassed by line managers to lodge a complaint outside their department – perhaps with personnel or a much more senior manager. Informal routes should be available in the first instance for resolving cases of harassment, but if necessary the disciplinary procedure should be invoked. Trained counsellors can help victims of harassment decide how to proceed, and also educate people of whose behaviour complaints have been made, especially if this behaviour stemmed from insensitivity rather than malice.

Both allegations of harassment and workplace affairs can create dilemmas for organisational decision-makers, as they tread the thin line between preserving individual rights and ensuring the welfare of the whole workforce. Such extreme cases might never occur in many organisations. However, it would be an unusual organisation which was not characterised by some level of 'banter'.

'Office banter' is a catchall framework for all manner of frolics and frivolity – and serious abuse. The 'office banter' line allows people like Philip to say that things are only a bit of harmless fun – a joke – a lighthearted pleasantry. It allows issues to be labelled 'not serious', and therefore not worth expending time on, feeling guilty about, taking responsibility for, changing. By the use of the word 'banter' sharp, significant matters can be blunted or obfuscated or lost.

Judy did not have a reasonable yardstick for acceptable levels of banter. Simon probably was bantering when he asked about her suspender-belt. He is, however, almost certainly not telepathic, and, without knowing her history, can only have taken her sharp retort at face value. He may have inferred simply that she is a prig (which she isn't) – or that suspender-belts are off-limits as topics of conversation for all women (which they aren't). He may have concluded that he was being intrusive (which he was). Philip, however, used the 'banter' label to disguise abusive behaviour.

So what's the answer: keep things clean by banning banter? Yet a banter-free workplace would be desperately cold. Proper banter is the irrelevant, friendly, funny stuff which makes routine palatable and crisis bearable. Increasingly, though, 'proper' banter subsumes improper banter – unthinkable twenty-five years ago when we were all Mr and Mrs and Miss, and much more ladylike and gentlemanly. As the formalities of working life have broken down, we all use forenames promiscuously; there is a tendency, exaggerated by the current emphasis on service enhanced by personal relationships, for us to behave in business more as pseudo-friends than colleagues; the taboos on things we can mention in mixed company have shrunk. So the field of potential banter-fodder has widened considerably.

All measures of offence are personal and idiosyncratic, as are people's courage and their capacity to do anything in response. If certain people said to me (at my age and in my state) that they thought I'd look wonderful in a black basque, I would be incredulous, but more gratified than offended. However, I was once outraged, horrified and helpless at an informal dinner on a course I was leading – just because a delegate used the phrase 'grumble and grunt' in a discussion of rhyming slang. It made me feel bad, so I ignored it, as did everybody else. So he said it several more times. Why? I don't know, and I wish I'd asked. Why didn't I – or anybody else – raise an objection? For my part, it was because I thought my dirty mind might be reading things into it and I could be wrong, or I might not have the right to feel bad about it; I felt it was a matter of more significance to me than to him, and that he would feel aggrieved if I made a big deal out of what, to him, was nothing. I had a professional role to fulfil and wasn't sure how to maintain it while still making my point as a woman. The rules of badinage are unspoken, so if you suddenly start speaking them you turn into a heavy, humourless spoilsport. So I didn't stop him.

At one end of the banter dimension there's priggishness, and at the other there is inappropriate licence. Somewhere in between is an organisation's banter bandwidth. Not everybody will be as happy with it as those who are happy with it think. Absence of complaint need not mean there is no cause. It would be a tall order – and death to spontaneity – to define the precise boundaries of acceptability within an organisation. You'd have to provide an index prohibitorum, a list of unacceptably lewd comments. Individuals could try amassing a collection of snappy replies to deflect banter of an unacceptable level. What should Robert have replied when Valerie, who didn't know him all that well, put her hand warmly on his thigh during a workship and enquired: 'Are you OK, darling, or am I making it hard for you?' What was Mary's best response when James, a senior manager who had met her for a business meeting a couple of hours before, turned to his three colleagues and called: 'Hey, guys, let's all rate Mary out of ten on the Moisture Factor!'?

Here, by way of inspiration, is an example. Eighteen words. An unanswerable putdown. Speed, subtlety, relevance, clarity, wit. No rudeness, no aggression, no challenge, no debate. Once upon a time two managers worked in the same company. The man fancied the woman very much. She made it plain that she was not interested in him, and his advances were not welcome. Finally, one day, in front of a number of male colleagues, he said to her: 'I really want to fuck you.' She met his gaze serenely and wagged a finger at him. 'Well,' she said, 'If you ever do – and I find out about it – I'm going to be *very, very* cross.'

Not everybody can think that fast. Those who can't still have the right to be confident that, if the need arises, they can voice an objection, and that their personal point of view will be respected, even if it is not endorsed. Banter is fine if you've agreed to play and have a say in agreeing the rules, and/or the right to object, or to opt out and take your ball home. Vulnerability is the issue. It's nearly always men who banter, and women who are bantered at, and the difficulty is that men's and women's standards are different. As gender groups they have their own sense of the boundaries of taste, good manners and appropriate behaviour. Swapping opinions formally and informally is invaluable because it enlarges the perspective for both sexes. Men are often surprised by what women class as unacceptable. In experiments, when watching a videotape of social interaction between a man and a woman, men were more likely to perceive the woman as having sexual intentions, whereas women were more likely to see her as being friendly. Men label fewer types of behaviour at work as sexual harassment, and have broader definitions of what constitutes acceptable social-sexual work relations. Men don't mind ambiguous situations which worry women. Many men find sexual overtures at work flattering; many women find them insulting. 'Harass me, girls! I'm yours!' says the Area Manager as he arrives at Head Office. There's no malice in it, but it's often a misjudgment all the same. Women are quite capable of harassing men, but it's less common, partly because they are not usually bold enough, partly because 'harassment' is not normally the name men give to what women do, and partly because it's more often men who are in positions of power.

It is important that members of both sexes recognize that there is a widespread mismatch. If they do, men are less likely to feel personally disgruntled because a woman is apparently making a fuss about nothing, and women, while preventing what they see as excess, can at least feel less personally threatened by it. In many organisations most managers are men. Without an appreciation that women see things differently, they may underestimate the impact of the prevailing culture, and act with insufficient conviction to change it.

Here's another story, in which a happier ending was ensured partly by the willingness of a group of men to accept the importance of the perceptions of female colleagues, align themselves as allies, and do something about a damaging situation. The story concerns a woman not as love-object, but as the almost random target of widespread sexual harassment.

## Blanket bombardment

Until recently Anne Eccleston was a Probation Officer with an assignment inside a men's prison. She talks of it now as 'an ordeal by fire'. Within the walls, she found, women fell into simple categories. The first distinction was whether they could – however loosely – be described as 'young and attractive'. If so, then they were treated as sex-objects. If they were not young, then they were classified as 'grannies', and if they were not attractive, as 'dykes'. Sex-object, granny or dyke: not a great field for manoeuvre.

Anne found herself in category one. Daily she ran the gauntlet of a range of remarks and ploys, from both inmates and staff. Catcalls and wolf-whistles from the prisoners were at the mild end of the range, but still cumulatively upsetting. A frequent remark was: 'What's a pretty young thing like you doing in a place like this?' Anne's reply to this matured over time. Her aim, she says, was to 'undo their perceptions, so that they would take me seriously and I could do the job I was being paid for. I'm blonde and I'm female, therefore I must be a pretty young thing. I used to reply: "But I'm forty, and married with three teenage daughters, and I've been doing this job for twenty years."' At the other end of the range was behaviour Anne describes as 'gutwrenching and humiliating stuff' – like the competition she heard of amongst staff at the prison to see who would be first to get her knickers off.

Anne saw the prison as a hothouse, an intense and undiluted version of what happens out in the real world. She tried to confront and resolve the issues as they arose by signposting them, explaining how she felt about them, pointing out the way they jeopardised her ability to do the job. What kept her going was her conviction that she was bringing something useful to the job, not only because of her skills, but actually *because* she is a woman, and could therefore represent half of the outside world within the single-sex community. The harassment she faced – both major and minor – was impersonally aimed at her as a symbol of her sex, but the target it struck was a very personal part of herself. It began to distort her self-image, and she could not ignore it. 'Ignoring or distorting the issue of sexuality gets in the way of the work that needs to be done.' She was forced to reassess herself as person, woman, worker and sexual being.

Initially Anne felt very alone, and very angry, but the Probation Service enabled her to work through the process by putting her in touch, at her request, with a senior female colleague who acted as a mentor and counsellor. Eventually she went on a professional development course. To her dismay nothing on the syllabus addressed the particular difficulties of the many women working, in various functions, in men's prisons. As women on the course got to know one another they learnt how widespread and how similar their experiences were. Yet their organisation was expecting 100 per cent professional competence without helping them overcome the obstacles to producing it. Indeed, they saw little evidence that it had so much as recognised the problem. The women set up their own seminars on the course, which resulted in a series of interconnected strategies which the organisation eventually adopted. These included distributing written accounts of women's experiences, keeping the topic permanently on conference agendas, involving the Union, encouraging the use of external counsellors, and creating internal support groups as a base from which to work.

One of the contributors to the seminars arranged by the women on the course was a man whose assignment was in a women's prison. He had similar stories to tell about his experiences there: the catcalls, his total humiliation. But whereas the women portrayed prison life as a microcosm of the outside world, he described the shock of immersion in a predicament which had previously been entirely outside his experience. Hearing what the women had to say helped him sort out his own perspective; however, Anne and her female colleagues were not totally sympathetic. 'I'm afraid it was almost: "Big Deal!"' she says. 'It made us see a connection between sex and power. Women in prison gang up and ape men's style. It's the only power they have.'

The turning-point for Anne was when she realised the problem was not just hers, but also belonged to her team and to the profession in general. The Probation Service needed to be consistent and united in its approach as well as its goals. This made the issue political, not personal. She got it on to her team's agenda.

She reckons she was very lucky in her team members. All – men and women alike – were sensitive and thinking individuals, prepared both to listen and to act. The chief role played by the team was to allow everyone to air and monitor their feelings. For Anne this was of paramount value in preventing her from becoming desensitised and hard, which had been the way she saw herself going. 'You get called "old slag" or "pretty young thing" often enough, and eventually in self-defence you learn to turn off the feeling of hurt and damage – but you stop being outraged as well. Other members of the team help you deal with the hurt without ignoring its cause.'

The men in the team also came to need the team's support. They re-evaluated their own behaviour in the light of what the women said, and decided they should contribute to the consistency of the overall approach by abandoning behaviour which might cause offence and hurt. This forced them to act in ways which conflicted with the prevailing culture. Because they did not toe the gender line, they met scorn and puzzlement from prisoners and prison colleagues. Were they proper men, or weren't they? (Not so much 'the Welfare' as 'the Welfairies'.) This made them, too, prey to discomfort and self-questioning. They were not themselves primarily accountable for the damage that had been inflicted on their female colleagues, but made changes as representatives of the men who *were* responsible. They had to confront their own sexuality in a wider context. The men were not able to stop the harassment, but their support mitigated its effects, and there was an increase in the men's understanding of the women's point of view – and vice versa. Feelings became currency at meetings, and began to be valued as a strong influence on team decisions about a whole range of other items at work. This heightened the team's joint contribution to their other professional goals.

It was Anne's misfortune that, although the kind of verbal assault she describes is not at all uncommon, it occurs in a much more concentrated form in places where lots of men are locked up for a long time. The good news is that she encountered – or generated – a series of mechanisms for resolving the issues. Firstly, the Probation Service is one of the caring professions, with a built-in vocabulary for intangibles such as emotions, and experience in counselling and listening skills. In addressing the team's joint stance on sexual harassment its members simply had to turn their professional vocabulary and insights on themselves. There are many, many professions where such a procedure would be far less natural. If the skills exist in the organisation, brilliant; if not, professionals may have to be imported. Secondly, in contrast to

Judy, Anne had the benefit of solidarity with other women, and a strong enough message to make the organisation sit up and take notice. Finally, at local level, she had access to the team agenda, and to brave men who were prepared to make themselves vulnerable by behaving 'unnaturally'. Men who don't harass women may find it hard to believe anyone *could*, if only on the grounds of good manners. Many find it untenable to be tarred with the same brush as those who do, or to be held to account when they themselves are not guilty. Accepting the sins of the brotherhood as something they can help to change from within is a huge first step. Men who can, without defensiveness, accept that all this happens, *and* radically alter their own behaviour to help women, are wonderful allies.

This was an excellent example of how strong personal relationships between women and men at work could address problems, rather than create them. Solid inter-gender relationships at work add depth to communication and increase quality of performance. One Director was particularly conscious of the value of man/woman teams at work. 'I used to work for a woman fifteen years older than me. There wasn't any sexual attraction in it. She was a spinster, not a member of the drinking club, no funny jokes – proficient, directional, a brilliant director but a useless manager. I used to provide the fun and innovation in what would otherwise have been a staid situation. It works the other way, too. I had a secretary who came to me straight from school and was with me for ten years. She knew me inside-out: the job, the detail, my requirements, which way I would jump. She complemented my untidiness, she supplemented my speed. And I admired everything she did. When she left, it was like a divorce.'

Like this man, people often make the connection between home and work relationships. One positive transfer of habits from outside to inside organisations exists in the phenomenon of 'office husband/office wife' couples – sometimes, rather ponderously, called 'non-sexual love relationships at work.' Sex may be out, but gender is a crucial factor. Man and woman are not just pals who enjoy one another's company, like a pair of single-sex mates, though there's that too. Support is reciprocal, but different. They act as peer mentors, using their perceptions of the world as filtered through the framework of their gender to interpret it for the other working partner. For the 'office wife', it's the relationship from which you get your unpatronising feedback about the way you relate to others at work and the length of your skirt; it's where you get permissions if you temporarily can't manage them yourself: permissions to be confident, to be assertive, to behave naturally. For the office 'husband', it's the source of new slants on tired old business issues, which take account of the intangibles such as emotion. Such a relationship demands mutual trust and a big enough fund of solid goodwill to give and receive bad news, and to weather the moments when either or both forget this is work and start behaving more like standard domestic spouses than working colleagues – tiffs and all.

The work/home crossover can, of course, create difficulties of its own. The way people view their relationships at home influences their behaviour at work and vice versa. Often work relationships are described in terms which echo private dynamics. One retail manager thinks a man's secretary represents an ideal combination. 'Often men treat their secretary as the wife they would *like* to have: sexy – and sackable.' Warm non-sexual relationships may have to be treated with discretion. Andy, a distribution manager, talks fondly about the excellent working relationship he has with his second-in-command. It's productive as well as fun, and makes work something to look forward to. Andy is a man with a great capacity for affection; he and his colleague value each other very highly, and give their company good value for the eight hours they have 'company permission' to spend together. 'But I couldn't go home and tell my wife about it,' he said. 'I always play Jean's role down.' 'Why?' I asked. 'Because she wouldn't understand. She would think there was more to it. She'd be jealous of the time I spend with Jean, and she wouldn't believe that I could have fun and get the job done at the same time unless I was involved in some sort of romantic liaison with Jean.' Andy has to behave at home, he feels, as though part of his team at work were less valuable than it is.

Donald, another manager, has a linked problem. He is not happy with either of the close relationships he has with women. 'The shit I get from Claire at work reminds me of the shit I get from Cathy at home.' However, he feels he can't discuss it with Claire as he might with Cathy. Whereas at home the relationship with Cathy is the goal, at work the goal is the task, and the relationship merely a means to an end. Anyway, in Donald's view, you just don't talk to working colleagues about any personal irritation you feel. He feels he can only talk to Claire if they are wearing their 'manager' and 'subordinate' hats; but those hats don't fit, because it's a gender-rather than a task-based concern which is causing the trouble.

Other domestic relationships can influence behaviour at work. Family dynamics can map on to work hierarchies. Managers talk about 'the girls' as they might at home about 'the kids'. Sometimes it works, sometimes it doesn't: it depends on the way it's put across and perceived. Jealousies, affections, obstructions, rivalries may echo some of the dynamics we grew up with; and trouble can arise from the translation of particular modes of behaviour into an inappropriate context. People end up transferring skills gained by habit and practice from role to role. For instance, women often spend years practising their leadership, management, counselling, discipline and support skills on beings under two feet high – what happens when that transfers badly? 'She comes to the weekly meeting, always late, and says "Hallo, children, how are you?" Pathetic. She's more like a nanny than a manager.' But nobody's told her. So she keeps on doing it. Domestic partnerships between men and women sometimes founder on deepseated (and 'forgotten') experiences of how it was when you were a toddler. It's just the same with some relationships at work. An elderly accountant said he found women in business 'tough and unremitting' – and compared them with the matron at his prep school. Absolute power, omniscience, an all-seeing eye, from which there is no hiding-place. Women in authority can prompt profound feelings of resistance in both men and women, because they are reminded of when they really were small and helpless, and totally dependent on Mummy.

Nobody would pretend that there is not a range of pitfalls in relationships between men and women at work. The responsibility for minimising them and increasing the benefits belongs partly to individuals, and partly to the organisation they work for. Organisations must define which problem areas are properly their concern, set up procedures to deal with them, and monitor the results. They might offer training, to enable men and women to understand how their perceptions differ, and to be reassured that noting and discussing them is a contribution to general morale, not evidence of sexism. Teasing out unwritten codes and opening up ambiguities increases understanding and tolerance, and therefore minimises destructive behaviour which hampers work performance. Men, in particular, need help in anticipating more accurately how others will perceive and react to their behaviour. Sometimes separate men's and women's support groups can be useful for airing really awkward points more safely at first. Managers need counselling skills which include a sensitive and informed approach to gender issues, and an understanding of the boundaries of their own competence to advise others. Formal mentoring arrangements are also helpful. By underwriting such formal activities organisations demystify their part in creating an environment which will foster positive relationships between people. From then on, informality takes over, and it is down to individuals to behave constructively, using any insights available to them.

Good relationships at work generate benefits beyond enjoyment of getting on well together. They contribute to overall morale and productivity, and re-channel energies otherwise wasted on speculation and irritation. Moreover, anything which women and men learn about assessing and adjusting their behaviour towards one another can be transferred into other areas. Roles and relationships at home affect attitudes at work: it's at least as likely that positive and valued relationships in the workplace will influence what happens between people outside it.

PART TWO

# What's to be
# done about it?

# 7 Narrowing the Acceptability Gap

We seem to have reached a point of disarray. What have we got? A lot of negative feelings about men, women, the gender issue and everything that could conceivably be contributing to it. Women and men are unsettled and confused about what's happening and why. It's serious, it's frivolous, it's a war, it's a game, it's low on the priority list, it's not happening, it's not my problem, it's not my fault, I can't be bothered, they're cramping my style, it makes me sick. Some of these things are said, some unsaid. Either way, there's not enough action, a shortage of results. Women aren't being judged on merit, don't succeed in putting their case across, aren't convinced that the values, culture and practices of their organisations are the best that could be devised. Men aren't sure what to expect, don't always understand what they see, aren't clear about the benefits women offer at work.

Yet at the same time, beneath the resentment, the resistance, the frustration, there is a groundswell of puzzled goodwill, tinged with cynicism. What is missing is a sense of excitement. The workplace is in a state of unhappy disequilibrium, from which there is no going back. In the interests of effectiveness for individuals and productivity for organisations all this needs to be resolved. People can't afford to be at loggerheads over something they spend a third of their waking lives doing together. We can consider segregation of the sexes, or limp along with a one-sex workplace – or sort it out.

## Initiatives

In some organisations much is being done to give women a fairer deal. Opportunity 2000, the national campaign launched in 1991 to increase the quality and quantity of women's participation in the UK workforce, highlighted existing programmes and prompted new ones. Sixty-one companies signed up at the start, and in the ensuing twelve months they were followed by another seventy-odd, less in the pursuit of justice than for reasons of sheer good business sense. Signatories aren't (necessarily) altruists. They accept a number of strong commercial reasons for boosting the place of women in their organisations. The key five are summarised in *A Balanced Workforce?*, published by the Ashridge Management Research Group as part of the Opportunity 2000 campaign.

- Subscribing organisations wish to be attractive to a large pool of the best people in a radically changing environment; they require an adaptable workforce, including part-timers and people on contracts.
- They want to get closer to their customers, and consequently be more attuned to changing customer needs.
- They recognise that costs can be saved or reduced. Breaching equal opportunities laws can let a company in for substantial fines; more important than this, however, is the lost investment. Highly trained women who take their skills elsewhere need to be replaced, and the recruitment and training process is expensive in time and money.
- They want to capitalise on the value of differences. Groups of people with very different backgrounds are sensitive to a greater range of possibilities than groups whose members have more in common. This presents a better chance of producing something new: new products, new solutions.
- And they are planning for a balanced organisation. The most enlightened companies have a fundamental belief in the individual, and regard it as a vital task to develop all their people to their full potential.

The practical initiatives organisations undertake can cover a number of angles. Here is a brief run-down of a selection, many also taken from *A Balanced Workforce?* They divide into three main categories: getting a consistent Equal Opportunities policy firmly on the agenda, with monitoring systems and measurements; taking positive action to increase available resources for women at work, and to eliminate sources of bias; and adding flexibility to the working routine.

## Getting equal opportunities on the agenda

- *Giving initiatives a name.* The Equal Opportunities statement for Rank Xerox is 'We discriminate only on ability.' The BBC call their programme 'Reflecting the Nation We Serve'.
- *Integrating the Equal Opportunities statement into the Business Plan.* The Littlewoods programme has been under way since long before Opportunity 2000, and follows a five year rolling Equal Opportunities plan included in the Business Plan, involves targets set by managers and the company's Equal Opportunities Unit, and is supported by a Code of Practice and appropriate training.
- *Equal Opportunities awareness-building events.* These generally start with the top echelon, and move further into the company.
- *Targets.* The BBC's target is to increase the number of women at middle and senior management level to 40 per cent and 30 per cent by 1996, from 18 per cent and 10 per cent. The National Health Service target is 30 per cent women in general management posts by the end of 1994, from 18 per cent in 1991.
- *Information and monitoring.* The Civil Service in Northern Ireland monitors men and women who attend training. The TSB Group companies submit progress reports twice a year on Equal Opportunities, and each Chief Executive is accountable to the Group Chief Executive for results.
- *Employee Attitude Surveys.* These are undertaken by many large companies. For instance, in 1992 Texaco commissioned the Industrial Society to canvass its employees about their views on Equal Opportunities as part of the Opportunity Texaco initiative, which is designed to address all areas of discrimination, including gender, race and disability. The survey was devised to identify direct and indirect bias, and provide a benchmark to measure progress towards its Equal Opportunities objectives.
- *Partnership with Unions.*
- *Attention to public relations material for use outside the organisation.* It should be relaying the same message as internal material.

- *Providing a central forum for monitoring the issues.* The National Health Service created a Women's Unit in 1991 which works closely with the Equal Opportunities Commission. One of its achievements is a register of women who want to compete for very senior posts.

## Positive action to provide resources and eliminate bias

- *Including women on recruitment shortlists wherever possible.*
- *Training managers in interviewing skills.* The Co-operative Bank trains managers in 'competency-based' techniques to eliminate bias at recruitment interviews, and Legal and General has introduced 'gender-neutral' procedures for appraisal and assessment.
- *Women-only training.* In 1985 the Sims Report recommended training for women only at the BBC. The BBC had earlier resisted it, on the grounds that it would create a ghetto, but became convinced that it would improve women's confidence and assertiveness, and alleviate feelings of isolation at senior levels. BBC Scotland has reported on the success of the residential, non-residential and private study training courses it provides for large numbers of its women managers and non-managers.
- *Ensuring that questionnaires and tests used in selection and promotion processes are neither gender- nor culture-biased.*
- *Providing common terms and conditons for all staff.* This move is intended to counteract the historical tendency for part-timers – mainly women – to earn less than the full-time rate for the job, and to be subject to less favourable terms than full-timers.
- *Tightening up Job Evaluation Procedures.* This is to ensure that, where jobs are not identical, a fair assessment of 'equal pay for equal value' is made.
- *Written policy on sexual (and racial) harassment.* Policy statements are made available to all staff, defining harassment and outlining how to make a complaint.

## Increasing flexibility

- *Job-shares.* These can work very smoothly, but there is sometimes cultural opposition. The BBC have offered job-shares since 1979, but only 100 of their 28,000 employees opted for it in 1992.

- *Flexible working*. Littlewoods and Boots offer a term-time working scheme; during the holidays students fill in. Other organisations offer working from home and temporary contracts. Companies start by auditing all their jobs to establish where flexibility is possible.
- *Family leave*. The Midland Bank's Equal Opportunities Director maintains that you can't change business culture until you accept that men too need to be included.
- *Career breaks*. Child-care is one purpose for which these are provided, but other examples include education (The British Council) and voluntary work (The Body Shop). 'Keep-in-touch' schemes are also provided by some organisations to women who take maternity leave.
- *Programmes for re-immersion after career breaks*. Avon Cosmetics Ltd have an Equal Opportunities taskforce which is spearheading a development programme for women returners.
- *Providing child-care*. Bradford City Council run a nursery, having found that the cost of replacing the staff who would leave if it closed would be much higher than the expense of maintaining it. Avon Cosmetics Ltd give financial support to the Pre-School Playgroup Association in addressing back-up for working parents.

It may be that the British are particularly insular. Professor Juliet Lodge, nominated 1992 Woman of Europe for her efforts in accelerating European unity, certainly thinks so. Quoted in the *Guardian* of 22 April 1992, she said: 'There is an extra element of misogyny and fear of women here which I don't encounter abroad . . . Our class-based society makes some British men more defensive or aggressive towards women.' Research published in October 1992 by the Department of Employment suggested that attitudes to equality in Denmark and Holland were most enlightened, and that France was more advanced than Britain. Company programmes in Europe and elsewhere provide an effective route to the identification of best practice. Initiatives reported from outside Britain include:

- *Acceleration*. IBM Sweden implemented a programme for women returning from maternity leave, who make up what they have missed by spending shorter periods of time than other comparable managers in the posts which they fill.

- *Communication packages*. Argyle Diamond Mines in Western Australia produced a recruitment and training video starring real-life employees.
- *Mentors*. In the United States women managers said that a key factor in their success was a male colleague at a higher level who acted as their sponsor.
- *Try-outs of work in other areas of the company*. In the States, men and women may be offered the opportunity to spend time in other areas, and this helps break through gender-stereotyped roles.

Changes in organisational working methods are also taking place which may contribute to more flexible work patterns, although they are not aimed specifically at an Equal Opportunities target.

- *'Portfolio' working*. A phenomenon boosted by the redundancies caused by recession: many professionals who used to be employed full-time by organisations have gone freelance, operate from home, and manage part-time projects for a number of companies instead of just one.
- *Home-working or Teleworking*. British Telecom announced in August 1992 that it was offering up to 8,000 of its management and professional employees the opportunity to work from home, with the same pay and perks, and a contribution to expenses. BT estimates that productivity increases by as much as 45 per cent when an employee works from home, and of course the company saves on overheads. Up-to-date figures on the extent to which which this currently happens don't exist, but a Henley Centre for Forecasting survey dating from 1986 suggests that only about half of those offered such a chance would feel inclined to take it. One disadvantage is that it halves the number of people a manager can supervise.

## Where initiatives fall short

Many initiatives are publicised, and to hear some reports of organisational response to the Equal Opportunities challenge you'd think the total integration of women at all levels is just around the corner. It isn't.

When Lady Howe announced the launch of Opportunity 2000, she made it clear that, all too often, Equal Opportunities programmes in companies were 'piecemeal and discretionary', and that one of the aims of the campaign was to give them a new coherence and attractiveness. It has done that, up to a point. The issues have acquired a measure of mainstream respectability and produced a modicum of awareness where it did not exist – which is something, but not enough. Reviews of progress have encouraged the exchange of ideas and best practice. Perhaps the emphasis has been rather more on fact-finding than on actively redressing the balance; however, surveys and audits are a necessary part of the early stages, to identify exactly what needs to be done.

By the campaign's first birthday, some clear obstacles to faster progress had been identified. Among the most important was the dilution of the message. The campaign has often had a negligible impact upon line managers, who remained ignorant of their own vital role in translating Equal Opportunities targets into action, and values into behaviour. Another disappointment was that, while by the end of 1992 the signatories to the initiative employed between them a quarter of the British workforce, some significant employers had not subscribed, local government being perhaps the most conspicuous by its absence. In two-thirds of member organisations, measurable targets had not been set, and the aims remained somewhat nebulous. This was true of many parts of the Civil Service. One senior woman was quoted in the *Independent* of 5 November 1992 as saying: 'Bureaucracies are immensely good at putting ideas like Opportunity 2000 into perpetual motion. It goes round and round and sweet Fanny Adams changes.' As far as commercial organisations are concerned, cynics have called Opportunity 2000 just another public relations exercise, a fashionable idea dreamed up by the Board to enhance company image at little cost.

More general factors can slow programmes down. It's always possible to find a reason not to change the way things are – and the recession has been one of the most salient. The Personnel Director of a large distribution company enquired: 'What am I supposed to do? We're not recruiting at the moment. I can see that women would be great as drivers – they're careful, and good with the customers – but we've got thousands of men doing our driving, and we're not going to sack them and replace them with women. I guess that's a rationalisation for not doing anything at all.' Organisations which despite limitations on recruitment caused by the economic climate still publish Equal Opportunities targets commonly set them four or five years ahead, so that there is a chance of seeing major developments. Companies which use the current employment situation to justify the lack of a specific medium-term policy on gender issues encourage procrastination and uncertainty. Training initiatives should be designed now, so that both men and women can gain access to non-traditional jobs.

Another brake on progress can be the complacency of members of the organisation. The Personnel Director of Royal Mail says that Equal Opportunities there are not as advanced as its employees think they are – which is why Royal Mail is stepping up its initiatives. He points out that, if the resolution of the issues is misjudged in a large, 'quality' company, the thinking in smaller, less sophisticated companies may be frighteningly reactionary. One symptom of such complacency can be narrow self-congratulation on achievements in the upper echelons of the organisation. Women at any level face the same range of problems. However, publicity about occasional success at high levels can distract attention from what is happening – or failing to happen – underneath.

Without the right context some elements of an Equal Opportunities programme can be counterproductive. Women who accept organisational offers of childcare, flexible hours and career breaks can provoke reactions of condescending envy or pity: one of the skewed outcomes of the philosophy which assumes that looking after children is solely a female responsibility. Such practical mechanisms can be perceived as either pricey and undeserved privileges for women, or nuisance add-ons which make it clear that women are special cases, victims, constitutionally disabled for the world of men, and commercially unattractive in the short-term. The organisation giveth – and it taketh away. By making it *possible* for more women to work, it can make women less *acceptable*. Only the provision of such opportunities to any employee, regardless of gender, is likely to narrow the acceptability gap, and incidentally make it more socially permissible for men to take on extended non-work responsibilities. 'Child-care is not a cost-effective option,' said the Personnel Director of a very large company. It might be if men showed they needed it, too. Attach the idea of 'working parenthood' to women only, and it's shooting equality in the foot. There should be assessments of work and family needs across the whole company – including senior management where it's likely that the old stereotypes are strongest. All this will require the reappraisal of organisational culture, including the value of visibility.

'Equal Opportunities in organisations are like a Greek holiday resort,' said a senior Personnel Manager. 'There's a lot of random building going on – and a few good bits, but a lot of incomplete foundations and showy parts that don't actually work.'

Yet it remains imperative to maintain the impetus, on all fronts: the economic, the practical, the psychological. The evidence coming in continues to paint a depressing background. Of all the EC countries, the earnings gap between men and women remains widest in Britain. Joanna Foster, chair of the Equal Opportunites Commission, said in June 1992: 'Sixteen years after the Sex Discrimination and Equal Pay Acts came into force, discrimination is still alive and widespread throughout Britain.' The latest report from the Commission showed a substantial rise in women's complaints about discrimination, dismissal for becoming pregnant, sexual harassment and pay. The increase was caused partly because there are more women in different areas of the workplace, and partly because their expectations are higher. An Institute of Management report published in November 1992 showed that, among managers, the Men's Club and the attitudes of colleagues were perceived as more of a block to progress than family commitments or childcare. One in five respondents said there were no barriers to career progress for women; 43 per cent highlighted the Men's Club, and 35 per cent the prejudice of colleagues, as against 17 per cent who found family commitments to be a significant barrier and 9 per cent who felt similarly about the lack of childcare. Ninety-two per cent of the men in the sample were married, and 86 per cent were fathers; 68 per cent of the women were married, and half had children.

The focus – pay, prospects, pregnancy – in different areas of the workplace may carry a different weight, but all aspects cry out for attention, and they are interdependent. It's no good providing practical help for women if it is viewed as an undeserved perk, no good for organisations to raise awareness and launch into a major culture change if they don't put their money where their mouth is.

It is obvious, then, that there is much, much more that organisations can achieve to ensure the highest possible quality of performance, including the fresh contributions that women can provide. Equally crucial, however, is the responsibility of every individual, man or woman, working or not, to contribute to the future. There are actions they must take, with or without an official context. Quoting survey results and waiting for improvement is not enough. Initiatives can supply the context, but it's individuals who make the difference.

## His and hers

For women the benefits are acceptability, and judgment on merit. But there's a long way to go. 'Yeah, I know,' said a (male) Personnel Director: 'The oppressors aren't going to make the running to enable the oppressed to come forward, are they?' Too true. Women may be *entitled* to the same degree of instant acceptability as men, but they have to struggle to get it. The starting point for women is further away from the goal, and the route is strewn with hurdles, tacks, water-jumps and false trails. Women have a bigger personal stake than men in making changes, and there's no way they can rely on universal or consistent support from anyone else. If women want to mould the workplace nearer to the heart's desire they have to be prepared to make substantial changes themselves.

What's in it for men? This is not an appeal to masculine altruism, which is welcome – but rare. There's no reason but unselfish generosity why men should consider making working life less problematical for the sake of women alone – but every reason why they should do it for themselves. They stand to gain: a working environment which is more creative, more varied, more challenging, more fun; the option, perhaps, to reduce the pressure of having to be the breadwinner; the chance to be there at family high points; more fruitful relationships with working colleagues, including women; the opportunity to leave behind a quantity of harmful psychological baggage. This is not a wishy-washy women's issue.

The two chapters which follow outline some of the changes which individuals can make. Chapter Eight is mainly for women, and Chapter Nine mainly for men. The chapters are closely interlinked, because every action has an equal and opposite reaction. Welding men and women into a more effective unit requires give and take. Individuals have to understand the significance of what their colleagues are attempting to change. Joint success lies in reaching the goal without anyone getting crucified for doing what's necessary on the way – or for making mistakes.

Each chapter begins with an account of some of the obstacles to change. Women need to identify and resist myths which can paralyse positive action. Men must learn to recognise a range of cop-outs which are often quoted as a way of exempting them from taking part. (To call them cop-outs is a charitable way of putting it: they are often rationales which disguise real hostility to women.) In each chapter there follows an indication of the most constructive mindset needed to make changes, and a selection of rules of thumb for achieving them.

The reduction of threat, and the beginning of enjoyment, start with people taking risks and noting the results. The benefits will accrue by degrees for both men and women. As more women jump on board, men and women can decide to resist the changes, opt out altogether, make them possible – or welcome them with open arms.

# 8 Women: A Gender for Change

*Part One: Five Paralysing Myths*

Women often collude with men in constructing a series of myths in the name of adaptability, conformity, and proving that we're all-right guys; but such myths obstruct our progress and keep us down and out.

**PARALYSING MYTH 1: Gender is only an excuse, or What Glass Ceiling?** A surprising number of men and women feel there is simply no public issue about gender at work; that the whole question of gender falls outside the boundaries of what any organisation is about. Organisations deal in work and money: the bottom line is objectively measured, the pound is sexless, projects are neuter. Men and women are equal, we're all in it together, the job's the job, and it makes no odds what sex you are, provided the task gets done – so why bring in irrelevancies to a perfectly straightforward deal? If gender's not a public issue, then the progress of women is a matter of personal responsibility alone.

June Davies, a customer service manager with a large company, accepts and enjoys the difference between men and women, but becomes impatient with any suggestion that wider issues of gender should be given anybody's serious consideration for a moment in the workplace. 'It's all to do with your success at the job,' she says. 'If you meet your objectives and enjoy the job, there's no more to say. OK, so some men say and do daft things, but that's their problem and you take no notice of them.' June sees dialogue between men and women in the workplace as strictly a matter of individual style, not a political bandwagon. Statements about fitness or capacity should be confined to personal achievements and noted on individual appraisal records.

June is not alone in believing this. In a 1987 study which compared male and female managers, Beverly Alimo Metcalf found that, if anything, the women tended to be more career-orientated and ambitious than men. She suggests that they had to be more motivated to combat greater obstacles and prejudices, and one coping mechanism was to take full responsibility for the fight – and for the success. Many women believe that the best way forward is to accept total personal responsibility. Then if we are disappointed in our progress, we must focus on weaknesses of personality, skill, or knowledge, and it's up to us to do something about it. If we try to attribute failure to a factor outside our control by bringing in gender, all we are doing is creating an alibi for mediocrity and under-achievement which absolves us of blame, and of the need to exert any effort. Each of us flies solo, and we soar or crash accordingly.

The Glass Ceiling – a term more familiar to the average woman than the average man, perhaps – is perceived by many as just such an alibi. The Glass Ceiling is the transparent barrier against which women knock their heads at certain levels in an organisation. They can see there are more destinations above it, but they can neither pass through the glass, nor shout through it. Many women who refer to the Glass Ceiling effect condemn it as an excuse rather than a reality. 'Women blame their sex for their own personal weaknesses,' says June. Sue Harvey, the Managing Director of Luncheon Vouchers, was described in the *Independent* of 27 October 1991 as 'no champion of women's causes', and quoted as saying: 'I think of myself as a person first and a woman second. I don't believe the Glass Ceiling actually exists. I think women sometimes create it for themselves.'

For years I agreed with the idea that work is a gender-neutral zone. When I'm at work, I don't wave a banner bearing the slogan 'Working Woman'. I'm just me, doing a job as well as I can. When things go wrong I assume it's down to me to put them right. I used to believe that successes and failures, enjoyment or depression at work, were entirely under my control. I'd love to believe it still. However, it no longer makes sense to me. In principle it must be right that we should take individual responsibility for actions and their consequences. However, if it's just personality that leads to success or failure, job satisfaction or discomfort, then why are the personalities housed in female bodies least represented in certain areas of the workplace or round the Board tables? Is it that more women than men have an unsuitable personality? If judgments are really made on merit and there are so few women at the top, then are most women lacking in merit? If gender is only an excuse, then presumably all the women who claim it isn't are natural losers, railing at fate.

But consider the evidence. Women are no less bright, no less keen than men. What men and women require of work is similar: a sense of achievement, responsibility, control, self-development, enjoyment, recognition and a living wage. Against a background of comparable motivation and ability is the tally of innocent misunderstandings, the wilful discounting of women's contribution, the problems inherent in the selection and promotion processes, the underestimation of the social and sexual undercurrents which cause discomfort among both women and men, the statistics and the research findings. In order to be successful, women have to be better than men. They are forced to perform to higher standards and under more pressure to develop an acceptable image and working style which isn't necessarily their first choice of behaviour. In November 1992, Gillian Shephard, Secretary of State for Employment, talked not only of the Glass Ceiling but of the Glass Walls which women encounter as they meet 'outdated and unfair' attitudes at work – even after a year of the Opportunity 2000 campaign. All this amounts to an environment which is not woman-friendly. Its existence militates against the notion that each individual woman should fight a lone battle. Given the facts, it's ludicrous to suggest that gender is irrelevant, and that gender issues should not be tackled publicly or collectively. Ignoring the impact of the environment and relegating total accountability to individuals prevents women from recognising the challenges they have in common, and confronting them together.

**PARALYSING MYTH 2: Highflyers prove there is no problem, or If Mrs T can do it, why can't I?** It's often a severe disappointment to many ordinary women in the workplace that some women at the very top simply refuse to contemplate the question of gender at all, often not even giving it the dignity of denial. They exclude gender as a term in the debate, because, so the argument goes, it would be unthinkable to ask a man whether his masculinity contributed to his success. The women are behaving as though the world really were as they would like things to be: taking equality as a given – but too soon. One fine day in 2050 the question of gender as a debatable issue rather than a source of strength may not need to be raised. However, given the evidence, a refusal to confront the issue at this stage seems somewhat perverse.

Top women who don't contribute to the issue are acknowledging something by its omission – a significant factor by absence. They're saying: 'Being female is not a factor in the game'. When Betty Boothroyd was elected first woman Speaker of the House of Commons, she said: 'Elect me for what I am, not for what I was born.' How on earth does she distinguish? She did not wish to be a token. But not admitting gender is throwing out the gifts of femininity as well as its fact. Being female *is* a factor in the game. Pretending it isn't jeopardises a rich source of organisational value. Problems may be sexless, but solutions can emerge from acceptably different ways of tackling them.

There may be admirable reasons for top women to discount the effect of gender. Yve Newbold, Company Secretary of Hanson plc, talked in the *Independent* in October 1991 about her reactions to not getting a particular job she applied for. 'I cogitated a long time about whether I had been turned down because I was a woman. But it doesn't help you to think that.' She's right. 'I decided it was much better to feel I might not have been suitable in some way, because then I could move on.' She's strong. To assume control of your fate helps you act positively. But to do it by accepting something negative about yourself (particularly if you suspect it may not be true) demands exceptional levels of self-discipline, mental energy, and high self-esteem. It requires exceptional women to take that route, and exceptional people of either sex are rare. Even studies of male Highflyers have been hard put to it to find many common denominators between them – except determination and varied experience (and, usually, a devoted wife). All the qualities male Highflyers need are prerequisites for females, too. And women may have to make starker choices: no children, no spouse. They may need more luck: complaisant husbands who will accommodate their lives to their partners' are less common than supportive wives. Both men and women need talent to make it to the top; for women, talent may need to be reinforced by outstanding strength and courage beyond anything required of men.

There may be alternatives to innate strength and courage which enable women to deny that gender is a factor. Some women may be lucky enough not to encounter obstructions met by others; too unobservant to register them; too thickskinned to be affected by them; readier than others to adopt protective colouring and mimic men. Or they may simply be self-seeking enough to prefer to remain members of an exclusive minority. At the moment there can be a built-in advantage in being one of very few women in some areas of the workplace. Exceptions suggest exceptional talent. There is a halo of perceived excellence around the Few. Of course, they have to live up to it after that, but it's a good beginning, provided it doesn't raise unrealistic expectations and set them up for failure. It threatens to be a short-lived phenomenon, though: once more women enter new or higher reaches of the workplace the minority halo will become spread more thinly amongst them, and lose much of its lustre. So exclusivity may be something to cling to while it can be made to last.

The existence of Highflyers does not prove that there is no Glass Ceiling or that all women can be solely liable for their own future. Highflyers demonstrate nothing about the regular 'working woman'. Women who get to the top, despite all the opposition, are necessarily exceptional, either because they're lucky, bold and brave as well as brilliant, or because they're insensitive, ruthless and egotistical. It is wholly inappropriate to take their analysis of their progress as a marker for the ordinary woman, ambitious or not.

We need to beware of letting the existence of female Highflyers paralyse the rest of us, sometimes in a wonderfully paradoxical way. 'Look, there aren't many women at the top. Must mean only a few women have what it takes.' Or, alternatively, 'Look, there are women at the top. It can be done, so no allowances need be made.' We can't do without female Highflyers. We need them to provide models for the future. It's glorious that no little girl in Britain will ever doubt that Prime Ministers can be female. But the role-models we need say: 'I had these problems, too, and it can be done', not: 'These problems do not exist, and you're on your own, chum' – which exacerbates the sense of powerlessness that many ordinary women have. We can't all be Highflyers, and there's no reason why we should be. But regular women do face challenges which regular men don't, and it doesn't do the regular woman any service to be thinking along the lines: 'If there's no Glass Ceiling and Mrs T can do it, and I'm not getting any further, then it must all be my personal failure.' 'I think women should help each other, if they can,' says Anna Turnbull-Walker, a solicitor and *She* magazine's 'Working Mother of the Year' in 1991. I agree.

To say gender shouldn't be a public issue is a proposition for the strong or the smug or the shortsighted. To say that every individual woman has sole responsibility for her own success or failure only works for the phenomenal or the fortunate. To act as though all opposition were based on rational assumptions, you have to be brave or blind.

Those of us who aren't Highflyers can fend off paralysis by accepting shortcomings in the environment as well as ourselves. This is not to deny accountability, but to suggest it should be shared, by everyone. The aim is neither to encourage second-best by discounting excellence, nor to make working life safe and reliable for average people. It is to make it *possible* for women who have the talent to perform proficiently, yet who are not brave, thickskinned, or specially articulate, and who choose not to turn into men.

**PARALYSING MYTH 3: They're all decent chaps out there, or Don't upset Daddy.** Wendy Miller, a young service station manager, said: 'It's not a general issue we should talk about, because talking about it makes people feel unequal and angry. We should just get on with it, and not make a fuss.' She is a quiet example of taking personal responsibility for a challenge. To her and to many women it means not taking up more time and attention than they think they deserve, or creating the discomfort of conflict for themselves, or risking inflicting pain on men by making demands, or having to face men's defensive reactions. Men also oppose 'making a fuss' – but it means something different. For men, a fuss from women is to be avoided, because it threatens the status quo. It's tantamount to an inflammatory trumpet-call to start the revolution, accompanied by lamp-posts festooned with male corpses – or, at the very least, supper not being on the table.

Women, on the whole, don't want to upset men, or attack them, or castrate them, or give them a hard time. A senior female manager says she recognises that she is, in a sense, a split personality. 'My bolshie side thinks I should get the men to realise what's happening and make them do something about it. Then my subservient side thinks: well, let it go, softly softly, they're all right really.' Women understand that many men believe they are on the side of women. They display the best of intentions. Some iron their own shirts, defer to women, make deliberate public attempts to affirm the validity of women's contributions. It's a tremendous treat to meet men who not only welcome women, but revel in their presence and enjoy the difference. Not accepting these men 100 per cent as partisans can seem to undermine and devalue all their efforts, and lead to ungrateful rejection of an honest offer.

But there are others who do need to be confronted. Alongside the decent chaps who supply true support, there are decent chaps who are not yet convinced that there's a case, and indecent chaps who generate an undercurrent of pure hostility. Some men do not want women on board, or they simply feel: 'Why bother?' It's rarely the chaps you are talking to who articulate such extreme views, but it might be simpler if it were. It's comparatively easy to respond to overt, unashamed sexism. It's the cryptosexism that's so hard to tackle, and the gentle denial that there is any problem.

The chief accusation which stops women rocking the boat is that we are seeing a gender issue which isn't there. Men may deny that what they do has anything to do with their gender, and affirm it's a matter of personality, or nationality, or mood. But we have to remember that in a man's world everything masculine seems normal to men. They don't necessarily see the common denominators which are a function of gender. As far as they are concerned, they have other perfectly good reasons for what they do. The influence of their gender is only visible to people who don't share it.

There is such a thing as giving too much benefit of the doubt. We connive at cryptosexism if we make too many excuses for men. 'Men are a bunch of MCPs – but they're so lovable underneath,' we say, tolerantly. 'He's so patronising,' we say, 'but his heart's in the right place.' 'He can be appallingly cruel, but that's because he's focused entirely on company performance, and certainly profit's showing an up-turn.' If we believe that people are a key factor in the success of organisations, and that women have much to offer, then refusing to confront issues with individual men simply lays up long-term ills. Unless we make it clear that what women think and feel is important, men have the right to believe they have no responsibility for the linkage of their fate with ours; and they can inflict a lot of damage on themselves, women and organisations by hampering the change process.

**PARALYSING MYTH 4: Born to be a lady, or Feminists spoil things for normal women.** 'It's a load of feminist claptrap,' said one accountant, point-blank. His argument was that talk of difficulties for women at work is not a real issue, but simply a tired catchall piece of political bumf for hardline radical feminists to pursue. If you pursue it, you must be a hardline radical feminist, which means you have disqualified yourself from deserving reasonable debate about your status, and are probably incapable of acting sensibly in the course of your work as well. The only issue is how to shut you up.

Many women, like me, are discomfited when we see ourselves reflected back from men or women who feel like this. Are we really strident, unreasonable, cold, tough and hard? No: it's only one more old-fashioned, misconceived, irrelevant stereotype, and it's time we learned to ignore it. If the word 'feminist' is used as a term of disparagement by men, we need to reframe it as an acceptance of women's effectiveness, a sign of concern that we are making progress, and refuse to allow ourselves to be sidetracked by negative connotations, old and new. If it's women who decry feminism, I, for one, need to remember that I did, once. It was because I didn't have the nous to question the right of men to take priority.

But I didn't get where I am today without a history of feminists kicking against the pricks. The achievements of the Women's Movement could not have been created by stealth. Women like me needed feminists to tell us loudly, and if necessary by giving up their dignity, that men were limiting our opportunities and keeping us away from power. I never stood at any barricade: I had neither the guts nor the insight. But I'm glad other women did. All I've done is slipstream along behind them. Ideally less courageous, softer-spoken women would have followed on and taken their places in a man's world – which should have been the end of it. But it hasn't happened and we're still plagued by the ironing, plus the new images unfolding of the frustrated and sterile career woman who is slightly off her trolley.

'When people won't listen in the first place, how loud do you have to shout to make a point? How ugly do you need to be?' said a colleague, who's as keen as I am to stay ladylike. Ugliness is in the eye of the beholder. If the beholder lacks empathy for women's standpoint, and is fearful of the results of their urge for equality, he is likely to characterise any activity as ugly. So be it. If we keep saying the same things, we are often accused of being boorish, banal or boring. There are two responses to this: to withdraw and apologise, or to riposte by pointing out that if enough change were happening we would not be forced to keep covering the same old ground, quoting new versions of the same old facts. We can start by suppressing the impulse to apologise. Feminism is still about ensuring that women get fair play so that they can be judged on merit. As far as I'm concerned it's less an end in itself than a staging-post to an integrated partnership between women and men. The debate still needs to be heard. It needn't be raucous, it isn't silly, and anyone can join.

**PARALYSING MYTH 5: Flexibility is its own reward, or the Pollyanna Position.** Pollyanna was a dear little girl in literature, who used to play the Glad Game. This involved waiting until something vile happened to you, and then looking on the bright side and saying how glad you were about it. It's on a par with 'mustn't grumble' and 'worse things happen at sea' and 'it'll all be the same in a thousand years' – a way of maintaining perspective and keeping sane when you don't get what you want and you can't see a way to change it. Very adaptive behaviour, up to a point. Pollyannas stay motivated by seeking satisfaction where they can get it, rather than where they know they can't. If they don't get offered the opportunities they deserve at work, they rejoice in the freedom this gives them to devote more attention to the family. However, they may also be queering the pitch for less complaisant mortals, by making it unusual to challenge the set-up; and at the same time, by accommodating themselves to the situation rather than trying to change it, they are contributing to the next round of organisational failure to respond.

Always accepting apparent givens and making the best of them ensures stagnation. Taken to extremes, the Pollyanna Position can lead to too high an automatic assessment of goodwill, and too weak an intention to improve on circumstances. Together they can create a condition which looks dangerously like complacency. One example of an area where complacency on the part of women may be dangerous is the demographic trend. 'Women are a precious resource when there is nobody else' is not quite so cut-and-dried a proposition as it looks. It's likely that organisations will themselves be damaged when the economy settles down if they haven't made arrangements to harness the resources they need; this must be a spur for them to make their workplace more accessible to women, and the number of women in the workplace must increase. But there's no guarantee that it will be in challenging and interesting areas. Organisations may decide, myopically, just to muddle along, or to perpetuate the current state of affairs, in which women are already at the bottom of the pile – in terms, for instance, of pay and conditions – even though so many of them are working. If more women are needed, it is quite likely that they will be encouraged to join at similarly disadvantaged levels. It won't be enough for any woman to sit tight and wait for companies to knock, panting, at her door. Women need to take action at local level, by seeking out and maximising opportunities, and by valuing their services at a higher price.

Is there a generation gap? Are the younger generation more likely to be boat-rockers than the older one? It's often said that the newest working generation are not inhibited by expectations of gender-appropriate behaviour such as I grew up with, and are therefore less prone to paralysis than women of my age. However, there's another school of thought, which suggests that, because women entering the organisational world now have fewer barriers to leap than their pioneering mothers and aunts, many of them are, in fact, less confident and less articulate than the self-selected women of twenty years ago, who were sure they had to make a statement about breaking into a man's world. The Principal of St Hilda's College, Oxford – still a women's college – certainly believes that current intakes of students behave less assertively than their mothers' generation. A female assessment consultant agreed. 'Young women may sound more in charge of their destiny, but there's no more substance behind it now than there has ever been. They have high expectations, which they act on; but they haven't yet hit the problems of balance and organisational culture.'

In any case, it's quite hard to make waves at lower levels of organisations, even though the accumulation of difficulties quite early in their careers makes some women want to speak out in their first expression of discovery. Two young women described the situation in their professions. A barrister explained: 'There's a psychology of terror at the Bar. It's bred into the system, so you have to curb your tongue to get in there, to succeed. You can't tackle it at the earliest stage or you won't get any further in your career. You have to play the game – it's very galling.' She feels she has to ride a lot of punches in solitude, without support. A Detective-Constable concurred: 'You have to accept you are going to take a lot. You can't make many ripples as a DC: there would have to be mass action. If you go it alone and stand up for your rights you make a lot of enemies.' Both these women find it more expedient to accept the unacceptable than to point it out and fight it off. They certainly have higher expectations than I did at their age. The question is: will their expectations be met any more than were those of my generation? I predict that by the age of thirty they will be as confused and disillusioned by the pressures as any older woman now, unless they take their own steps to initiate change.

## Part Two: Cultivating a positive mindset

### INCREASING CONFIDENCE.

**Accentuating the positive.** Women have a lot to offer. The first people they have to convince are themselves – and then the people who make the decisions about recruitment and promotion. Women need to be able to rely more consistently on feeling confident and behaving accordingly. There are obstacles enough in this race without adding a burden of self-inflicted difficulties. Women must not only stop looking for ways to undermine themselves, but also identify themselves with the general business case for women in the workplace, and translate it into a formula which fits.

**The business case for women.** The important thing to the organisation, if we're trying to convince it to behave differently, is what we're offering. According to one male decision-maker in a large organisation: 'My instinct is against all this. Am I desperately bothered about the issue? No. Am I motivated to increase the numbers of women? No. Am I relatively selfish – wanting the best person for the job on behalf of my company? Yes. I'm very careful these days about how people fit in with the team. Not only ability, but a balance of age, experience, background. Convince me that having women on the team will enhance teamwork and team output, and already I'm listening closely. In other words, what's in it for me?' The way to a decision-maker's heart is to convince him or her that the result will be enhanced value, and that the instinct of conservatism means no advance.

The business case for women is moving away from an emphasis on equality, and towards an appreciation of the benefits of diversity. On top of whatever skills and talents women may have, they bring a different perspective to business challenges, and add a fresh element to the pool of resource within an organisation, from which new kinds of solution can emerge. Such an offer is far more commercially appealing than a straight call for justice.

But we don't have to give evidence of our abilities in the way men often express theirs (or cover up their insecurities) – by being aggressive, taking up a lot of air-time, pursuing power and dominance rather than constructing personal relationships. It's true that many successful top women managers adopt a comparatively masculine style, because it suits a man's world. But it's a mistake to mimic men. Men are better at being men than women are, and women's value is in bringing something new. An environment in which women don't have to mimic men demands greater idealism from us all, and a more open mind in defining success.

**Redefining 'The Lost Slice of History': Skills.** Many women – particularly of my generation – who would like to get a job have to persuade themselves first that they have something to offer. Needing money is a great incentive to convince potential employers that you are just what they require; nevertheless, it is sometimes difficult to redefine yourself as anything other than a housewife and mother.

Jerry Cope, Personnel Director of Royal Mail, says: 'Women returners have lost a slice of history. They're like male newcomers: they haven't got a background of events.' This is only true from the organisational point of view. Women returners have crammed whole episodes of history into the years they have not been in paid employment, and that experience will have led them to a maturity of judgment and understanding that needs only to be channelled to be perfectly applicable elsewhere. If timidity and self-abasement take over, women find themselves thinking: 'The things that have to be done must be very difficult and valuable. I haven't done them, so I probably can't do them. The things I can do can't be worth doing, because I can do them.' If they cultivate positive thinking, they say: 'I haven't done this *yet*, but I've done lots of things like it, which fresh-faced young men straight from college have not.'

Anyone who has persuaded a recalcitrant three-year-old to speak nicely to Granny, stopped hostilities between rival siblings, balanced the conflicting demands of kids, spouse and in-laws, taught a baby to talk, produced cricket teas, assisted at school, or convinced a teenager that a twelve-inch pelmet won't do for school uniform, can't help but have several of the skills which organisations need. They include: networking, selling, prioritising, crisis management, balancing your life, communication, negotiation, team-building, arbitration, conciliation, assertiveness, training and interpersonal skills. These skills may not have been acknowledged by diplomas, or practised at high or stretching levels – but they have been practised. They are all at a premium in today's organisations – and can be deployed by women, if they wish, to a wider audience than themselves and the baby.

The emphasis in organisations is moving from formal structure to informal open communications. The kinds of interpersonal strength that women have are not optional extras. They can help construct the new kind of organisation, rather than being confined behind the doors of the Personnel department. Ask people in any company how they want to get the news they need, and they'll say face-to-face from the people they work with. Managers are relying less on titles and status to get things done, and more on personal credibility by results. Interpersonal skills and the ability to tune in to unspoken messages are often crucial in getting to grips with what really matters both to customers and colleagues.

**Redefining 'The Lost Slice of History': Experience.** The BBC's Equal Opportunities initiative is called 'Reflecting the Nation We Serve'. Or, as Virginia Bottomley, the Health Minister, put it: 'To make sense of the Patients' Charter, regions need someone who has sat with a two-year-old on their knee in a hospital waiting-room.' A young barrister makes a similar point: 'Lawyers should be as diverse as their clients. I saw a male judge refuse to return a child to its mother because he said she had brought the situation on herself by living with a man like her boyfriend. It's scary to think of people's lives being in the hands of people like that.' Organisations and professions are currently focusing heavily on relationships with their customers. It's no longer enough simply to supply what is asked for. Sensitive and proactive handling of colleagues and customers leads to higher productivity and larger sales. Organisations are beginning to realise that running a household, and actually being a customer, puts you in touch not only with many other women, but also with the butcher, the baker, the candlestick maker, nurses, teachers, the Gas Board, and the Post Office. All these contacts give an understanding of what's behind the scenes and encourage empathy with people from a variety of backgrounds. Such experience is assuming a higher value in the workplace.

## COMBATING SELF-DEMOLITION.

**Guilt.** A middle manager with a challenging job and two young daughters can't help speculating: 'I wonder sometimes – am I letting the girls down? Have I damaged them by not being there all the time? When I'm at work, I'm sometimes distracted; it makes me feel very disloyal to my employer. But I can't help it. I'm torn right down the middle.' The stress of straddling two worlds needs to be addressed, not simply suffered. We need to decide what we are prepared to give up, make appropriate arrangements, and trust to our own decisions rather than constantly replaying them. If the responsibility can be shared with a partner, it should be. And when we do (occasionally) reassess the situation, we need to take into account both sides of the balance-sheet: we may have lost some positive assets because we do what we do, but we have also lost some liabilities.

**Fear.** We have to start somewhere, but we don't have to conquer the world on Day One. If fears of exposure or inadequacy are a burden, it's important to remember that, to get anywhere, one step at a time is enough. Elizabeth Neville, Assistant Chief Constable of Sussex Police, says: 'I could only ever see clearly what the next job entailed, and had an idea about the one after that. I don't think anybody can see clearly more than one or two rungs ahead up the ladder.' Goals shift with time and opportunity – and the skills which will be effective in achieving them develop with experience. As reported in the *Sunday Times* on 19 January 1992, the Deputy Leader of the Labour Party, Margaret Beckett, started off, like so many women, with an interest in people. 'I had gone into politics because I thought things needed to be changed, and because political decision-making underlay all the caring professions, like teaching and social work, which are really to do with helping people.' You don't have to be able to see the end of the road to step on to it.

**Pain.** It can feel painful to meet hostility, conflict and opposition at any point in working life where there is no consensus and a decision has to be made. Women often don't want to fight, and generally they want to be liked. The temptation is to soften disagreements so as to make themselves feel better – but, sometimes, this is not the best value they can give. It may be disagreement which produces new ideas. And, in any case, unexpressed disagreement is still there and can leak and cause discomfort. Unresolved baggage clutters up forward movement. Life at work cannot be expected to be a permanent source of sweetness and light, but nor should we assume that opposition is necessarily directed at us personally, whatever it feels like. It may simply be the message that is not going down too well – but an unwelcome message may still be right.

**Luck: be grateful for it – and then take the credit!** It's an excellent thing to be grateful for luck. However, we also need to recognise effort as our own, and not put all our successes down to Providence.

## Part Three: Rules of Thumb

**BUILD A SUPPORT NETWORK.**
**Get as much support as you can, wherever you can.** You can't have it all, but if you want a lot of whatever's going, you're better off with support, both practical and moral, in a variety of different areas: at home, at work, with other women, with men. Women's confidence can be substantially enhanced by personal support and encouragement.

172 Making the Difference

**Share chores and excitement at home.** If I could replay my adult life, I'd retreat earlier than I did from the traditional expectations of women as the mainstay of the family. I'd introduce family teamwork about ten years earlier than I did. Forget the Super-woman experience – everybody needs to muck in. I'd spread the chores and stress, but I'd also try not to hog *all* the pride and joy: number one son (aged five) singing Little Donkey in the village church, or number two son (aged nine) winning the non-swimmers' swimming race. Interlocking work and home can bring great pleasure. My sons and I keep each other going as we labour at the same table – they on their school projects, me on my reports. The boys have seen both parents on ecstatic work-induced highs and desperate lows. They already know a lot about how adults spend their time, and there are some facile assumptions they won't make when it's their turn to get a job.

**Whinge to women (sometimes!)** The glory of female support is that you can share the bad times – and women understand, and don't accuse you of griping. Women can be very strong, but it helps to express how bad things are as a way of getting through them. Where some men will often translate a story as evidence of helplessness, abrogation of accountability and inability to take control – and others will tell you forcibly what you should be doing about it – women find it more natural to provide comfort. Bouncing experiences against others enables you to test reality, and decide how much of what's going wrong is within your power to change.

**Don't collude in maintaining the status quo.** Women are usually the ones who provide central services to partner and family. They may be happy to do so. If not, it's no use complaining about the ironing if you routinely do it all, or about your husband's unreason-able expectations if you keep preparing his lunch-box. Aristo-phanes, the Greek dramatist, told the story of Lysistrata and her friends, who in 411 BC influenced the outcome of war by banishing their husbands from their beds until the men agreed on peace terms with their opponents. This may be going a bit far; it should, however, be possible for women to do their own ironing and lunch-box (but nobody else's) and face the consequences, even if they are uncomfortable.

**Find a male mentor or ally at work . . .** Because of my uncertainties in a working environment peopled largely by men, I'm very conscious of a constant need for reassurance. It's as though I needed permission to do things my way. Supportive male colleagues help by giving me that permission. I believe that, because of where we are starting from, many women will need to begin by getting reassurance from men they can trust and rely on for support. Gradually we will learn to give ourselves our own permission. This is different from allowing even sympathetic men to set our agenda and be sole judge of our activities. That is dependence, not alliance.

**. . . don't punish him . . .** There's a big trap here. If a woman finds a man who will listen, it is fatally easy for her, as she struggles to describe how she sees things, apparently to be viciously attacking him as a representative of his horrible tribe. Here's a classic response: 'I feel as though I've made a generous offer of my time and experience, and all you've done is criticise me. You claim you're talking about men in general – but what you actually say is "*You* do this and *you* do that." It feels like a bollocking I haven't deserved. I don't do any of the things you're talking about, but it feels like you're accusing me, not asking for a perspective.' Too much of this, and you've alienated your ally.

**. . . and don't let him punish you!** Somehow you have to make it clear (and he has to make the effort to realise) that there's no intention to punish him, by scoring points off him because he's open to debate, in revenge for points scored off women by men who aren't. He needs to know how much women value a sympathetic devil's advocate. He, on the other hand, shouldn't expect to be protected from the need to reassess his own behaviour. He's big enough and old enough to manage any defensive reaction he may experience.

**Build dialogue by being direct . . .** Being direct is fairer than expecting people to guess what's on your mind. They probably won't try, but if they do they'll most likely get it wrong. Tell them what you want, need, can't do with. Express it carefully, by building in explanations, such as: 'I want to be convinced of this, but I need reassurance.' Direct talk can deflect misunderstandings before they begin.

**. . . and insisting on feedback in return.** Indeed, support should be two-way – more of a dialogue. It's important both to get and give feedback. Some of this is appropriate within the formal structure. Appraisals are a good example. It may be necessary to reframe your manager's views, as well as your own, of what an appraisal is for. It is not just an opportunity to be reassured. Comments such as 'You're doing very well' are pleasant to hear, but unhelpful in giving signposts for improvement. Both men and women would rather be given an accurate combination of positive and negative feedback, than just positive feedback; but research suggests that women are more likely to receive global reassurance than specific clues as to how they can improve on aspects of their performance. So women may need to ask for them.

**Don't let anyone eliminate the negatives – we need them!** We shouldn't accept blanket answers to salve discomfort (ours or the appraiser's). We should actively test for evidence of mismatches between objectives and achievements, not for the security of 'No complaints'. No complaints means no learning, which means no progress. We should welcome painful answers. If we don't get them, we're either doing a spectacularly brilliant job, or only being offered comfort, and not ways to sharpen up. This may be because we are not regarded as strong enough to take criticism. So we have to be able to take criticism.

**Ask for training or experience to fill in the gaps.** Having elicited detailed feedback, we need to evaluate accurately what we are being told. Are our shortfalls in performance due, for instance, to absence of opportunity to exercise the right skills, or lack of professional expertise or experience, or inability to get hold of the appropriate information, or low levels of confidence and assertiveness? Only when we're absolutely clear on where performance needs polishing can we identify possible solutions to bridge the gap – and push to have them implemented. Training may be one answer. Women often aren't offered specific training which will bring them to a standard of performance which will add real value to the organisation. Indeed, many organisations do not keep full enough training records to monitor overall training requirements, let alone those which appertain particularly to women. Remember the vicious circle referred to earlier, in Chapter 4, in which, so research suggests, women are less frequently offered new projects, and therefore appear to learn less readily, and therefore are less frequently offered new projects . . . Clearly, the more experience that can be gained, the better for learning and development, so it may be necessary to keep asking proactively for projects or responsibilities.

## STEP OUT OF YOUR COMFORT ZONE.
**Who dares, wins.** Women need to dare a bit. Too many of us hate taking risks: speaking up, looking for opportunities to do something new. When I was a teacher there were opportunities to work in pairs or teams with colleagues, but I was always afraid of exposure, so I never took them up. Staying within your comfort zone shrinks you; moving outside it by degrees is enjoyable and stretching, and it gets easier all the time. Risks are often smaller in the execution than in the anticipation. But risks sometimes fail. We must expect some casualties, and then learn to face and deal with opposition without being demolished. A good support system is vital.

**If nobody tells you things – find out!** I've always been scathing about workplace politics, but I would no longer discount them. You don't have to play politics, but you need to be aware that others do, and to understand enough not to lose out. A Personnel Director maintained: 'The main element which holds women back is their failure to get enough information. This is often because they aren't there when the information is being transmitted. It makes them less able to deal with politics, which are necessary for quick promotions. They have less of a wish to play politics than men do, but they still need to respond, and avoid the traps, and they can't do that without information. They need to be reasonably sensitive.' If he's right – and I fear he is – then it may be necessary to ask point-blank for information which normally only trickles out, often in the pub, or after hours, in inner circles. If this is a shock to men's system, then so be it. Don't let them suggest questioning is naïve. It's necessary, if information is not forthcoming without it.

**Watch your language.** It's worth making a fuss about language. Clumsy and artificial though it seems at first, both genders need to be equally represented in speech and writing: 'he or she', and all that. This applies even before there are substantial numbers of women in whatever job you're talking about. What we don't want is contradictions like this one in an advertisement for a manager which appeared in the *Daily Telegraph* in November 1991, issued by a large British company: 'XYZ company is an Equal Opportunities employer . . . Candidates should have proven man-management skills.' Talk about 'man-management' often enough, and subconsciously the message is reinforced that it's men who are the natural members of the workforce. I met a purist who grumbled because his wife is a chair. 'Why can't she be a chairman or a chairwoman or a chairperson?' Yes, very awkward, but it's necessary to take the sex out of function titles, even at the expense of the English language. One day it will be both natural and realistic.

**Consider whether to boldly go where no woman has gone before.** Teaching, retail and psychology are all considered suitable jobs for women, and that's exactly why I picked them – because they were safe and comfortable, and I knew I would be acceptable in them.

But we don't have to do jobs that women normally do. There may be almighty antagonism to women breaking into new areas. According to a female Deacon quoted in the *Yorkshire Evening Press* in February 1992, much of the opposition to women being priests is based on the idea that 'Women are hearing God wrong' – they are not being called to the Ministry at all. For her part, she believes that female parishioners should have the option to make confession to another woman, if they need to hear that they are forgiven. A conviction that their offer is significant and necessary gives many women the strength to confront the inherited irrationalities of tradition.

**Don't limit the options too soon.** Tradition, stereotype and expectation can constrict women's options; but women themselves can also contribute to shrinking the frame. It's partly because women make limiting decisions early. It may be because they are resigned to the eventual restrictions a family will impose on them, and therefore set their sights low from the start. Or it may be that most of us are not cut out to be pioneers, and there aren't enough role-models. Or perhaps it is because we don't unpack stereotypes, but conform to them instead – as I did when for years I didn't think to challenge my partner's assumption that he was going to be the breadwinner. But it makes sense for women to widen their options where they can. If women want to make progress and be doing something more interesting in ten years' time, there are areas of the workplace where the odds are loaded against them before they start. Secretarial, clerical and selling jobs offer poor chances of reaching management – and they are all jobs that women go for in large numbers. In professional occupations, women traditionally take certain routes and men others: in law, for instance, fewer women than men opt for private practice, and women therefore are less likely to become partners.

**Apply for jobs you don't think you're worth.** 'I'd love to consider women for some of the more senior jobs we've got. But they don't apply. There's not a lot I can do if they're not in the queue.' It may be necessary for women to apply for jobs they don't feel confident about doing, let alone getting. Men aren't necessarily confident, either, but they are much better at acting as though they were. Women are too good at crossing bridges before they come to them. They need to put themselves forward – and, if they meet rejection, have the strength to put it down to experience.

**Cut your coat according to your cloth – or make them cut theirs.** You can't have it all, but you can have more of it than tradition would suggest. Taking time out of the workplace to bring up a family inevitably cramps your chances of swift progress. 'If you only have three promotions in you and you take ten years out you may miss one,' says Jerry Cope, Personnel Director of Royal Mail. True, so women need to be realistic, or convince potential employers that they can learn fast and have kept in touch, or that it is the company's responsibility to keep them in touch if it wants them back in six months or two years or ten.

**Play fair about PMT.** *She* magazine carried out a survey into menstruation and pre-menstrual tension (PMT). Fewer than a third of those respondents who take time off because of PMT are willing to give the genuine reason for their absence. It may be tempting not to tell the truth, either because the 'temporary lunacy' label is damaging, or because the subject is simply embarrassing. However, if it is a serious problem it ought to be addressed, and if women keep quiet about it an assessment of the true impact of PMT on women at work is impossible.

But it has to be kept in proportion. The context is confusing, and much of the evidence clashes. Assessments of the percentage of women who suffer from PMT vary wildly, from single figures to the high 80s. There is some evidence that women who have a negative attitude towards menstruation are the ones who suffer the most severe symptoms, which suggests that psychological as well as physical causes are implicated in the severity of the symptoms. Research into the experiences of 1541 Swedish women found only 83 who said they'd been absent from work during the previous six months because of PMT. But these women also showed more illnesses and absence from work for other reasons, and more mental disorders than the group of women who reported they suffered from PMT but didn't miss work because of it. PMT can be a hook on which to hang a load of other ills. Conclusive evidence has not been found to suggest that menstruation or PMT adversely affect work performance. (See also the section in Chapter 9 entitled 'You can't neutralise biology'.)

However, people should not come to work on days when they are so ill as to risk producing results which are under par, or physically unable to work, or likely to infect others, or there is any other overwhelming justification not to do so. These broad categories might conceivably cover men and women with flu, backache (one of the biggest factors keeping people off work), anyone with a sick child, people on regular dialysis, men with prostate trouble (who are also often shy about admitting it), the followers of some religions, insomniacs, people with hangovers, and those who are newly in love or who have just been deserted. Common sense, stoicism and strength of commitment help individuals make up their minds as to the best course of action. In the same way, each woman has to decide for herself in what category of severity her own symptoms fall, and whether the event is of negligible importance or tantamount to a disability. Giving PMT a name does not absolve women from attempting to control the results, however bad it feels physically or psychologically. If changes in behaviour caused by menstruation can be controlled, they should be; if they can't, then arrangements need to be made with employers as they would for any other disability.

**Try a different formula.** Lots of women are proposing term-time working, working from home, short weeks – and their offers are being accepted, because their employers have recognised the value they bring. If you want a job and more than just weekends at home, take the initiative and ask for a four-day week. Or find someone to do a job-share. (And men could try it, too. The first who ask may be given short shrift, but the more there are, the more 'normal' it will seem.) Concentrate on the benefit to the organisation – emphasise the value of your presence, not the problem of your absence. When there's balance between home and work, ideas stop being stilted because there are constant sources of fresh material, both ways. Proportion and perspective are maintained. These are the persuasive arguments.

## HANG ON IN THERE!

After Anne Eccleston and her colleagues gave the issue of sexual harassment a higher profile in the Probation Service, several initiatives were instigated at an official level. They all lost impetus *unless* women kept pushing for them.

In the *Independent* of 30 April 1992, Kate Adie, the television journalist, was quoted as follows: 'They said to us "Come on in", and then, years later, found we were still there, when, in fact, we were supposed to have a go and, having proved ourselves, go away.'

We have to keep on pushing. The price of inclusion is eternal vigilance.

# 9 Men:
# A Gender for Change

## Part One: Nine Copouts

Here are nine easy ways to avoid taking the issue seriously. They can be heard daily in the workplace, where they downgrade women, discount them, deflect them, ridicule them, or postpone their inclusion indefinitely. Copouts prevail where fear outweighs reason, conservatism rules, assumptions remain unquestioned, the focus is on cost at the expense of value and where people refuse to recognise real problems.

**COPOUT 1: Monstrous Regiment of Women.** I met Michael, a very senior Director in his late fifties. His main point, he said, was that there was simply no commercial need to make any changes. 'We don't have a problem; our line of business doesn't need women; it's built on areas which are strictly masculine preserves. Why bother to make it easier for women to enter the organisation?' Michael's (complacent) assumption is that practices which have apparently worked up to now will continue to work, and that no alternative could be an improvement.

However, the supposedly business-based conclusion 'We don't have a problem' turned out to be a façade disguising a passionate resistance to the entry of women, simply because they aren't regular chaps. Michael went on: 'Women are not advancing their cause by climbing into what men have already set up, forcing themselves into current structures, pressing claims on jobs done by men. It's counter-productive for them to muscle in on men's preserves. Why can't they find somewhere to use their own skills – invent a new profession where they can use what they are good at? Why can't they play to their strengths and not take up men's jobs – I mean jobs which have traditionally been held by men? Women are powerful matriarchs. Why can't they stick to their invisible influence, and stay off the bandwagon?'

Such attitudes are based on a ludicrously out-moded and unquestioning acceptance of a traditional sex-role split. Women are fine in their place, and their place is anywhere but here. Or, as the old joke goes: 'I don't discriminate against women; I'm married to one, ho ho.' The principle seems to be this: flatter women enough about their aptitude for power behind the throne, and it may deflect them from trying to mount the throne in their own right. Sometimes wives even reinforce the freemasonry, because it is their only means of access to power and prestige; collusion from women gives men permission to carry on in the old exclusive way. The daughters of this generation of men will, I suspect, only make much of a difference to their thinking if they were brought up in a reasonably liberated way in the first place. Michael's daughters are of an age to join the workforce. I asked him whether they had changed his view of women. 'No,' he said.

The tenor of day-to-day behaviour is governed by those at the top, and among many men at that level such attitudes are far from uncommon, although they are not always aired so candidly. At the time of the launch of Opportunity 2000 in 1991, its chair, Lady Howe, said: 'The problem is both attitudinal and generational. Many of the chairmen and chief executives still have wives with no careers. But perhaps as time goes on and they see family and friends with working wives, the attitude at Board level will change.' Her optimism will be well-founded provided that such men are forced to face up squarely to the need for the talents they deny, to their own fear of change, and to their anxiety about their own power if they can't maintain the artificial territorial boundaries which keep women in their place.

Men who cling to the attitudes prevalent in their earlier years are in for a shock. Viv Woodcock, Head of Equality and Development at Ealing Borough Council, says of her earliest years at work: 'We took inequality for granted: we expected less. Twenty years of feminism has made our younger sisters take equality for granted. They expect better, and usually they get it – and if they don't, they become angrier. But as each battle is won another one will open up. Each new generation of women will find new grounds for the fight.' New generations of men, too, are somewhat less blinkered than their fathers. Men who try to keep women in some notional feminine Elsewhere are bound to fail as they meet the challenges brought by less hide-bound men and women. But they can inflict great damage on themselves, women and organisations by turning the issue into a battle rather than a co-operative partnership.

**COPOUT 2: Time, Gentlemen, Please, or All things come to her who waits.** The next excuse for inaction is to assume that all evolution needs is time. Time is certainly an element. There's no doubt, for instance, that to be at the top of the tree now you need to have been at the bottom of it twenty years ago, and there weren't that many women there then. In twenty years' time things could conceivably be better for women, just because of the numbers of female entrants into the workplace now. But it's unlikely that the improvement will be major, if all we do is wait and see. If we're entitled to expect substantial improvement without effort, either women are already on an equal footing and all they have to do is take advantage of it – which is demonstrably false. Or some slow but potent magic will demolish all the obstacles to women's progress within organisations – and we really can't afford to wait ten or twenty years to see whether this (hopeful) reasoning is right, because we need the benefits of having women around much sooner.

Improvements don't just happen by osmosis or default, which is why the 'time' argument amounts to a copout. But there's more to it even than this. The 'softly, softly' approach can also disguise other, more egotistical motives for inaction, which Alec Reed, Chairman of Reed Personnel, describes thus: 'We suffer from ageism and protectionism. What we've got we don't let go. We've got the houses, we've had the gravy train, we've grabbed all the jobs, and we don't want to lose them.' Waiting for dead men's shoes ensures a workplace without challenge or experiment, where the only role-models are men. By no means a recipe for innovation.

**COPOUT 3: You've never had it so good.** 'Why are you still on about this?' asked a warehouse manager. 'It was an issue, but we've cracked it. It's now a part of history; the battle's long over.' Huge changes have, indeed, been achieved in our working lifetime; however, many of these changes are misleading. There are downsides which are not obvious, and the net result is a false sense of progress. Selective appreciation of aspects of the law, the media, the composition of organisations, may lull us into complacency.

It's true that legislation has been introduced – for instance, to outlaw unequal pay and discriminatory job advertisements. But companies get round it, if they choose, by using 'organisational restructuring' or 'rationalisation in time of recession' as their means of dodging the spirit of the law while holding to its letter. Moreover, maternity legislation proves such a financial burden for some organisations that jobs have been known to vanish as the women who hold them launch into maternity leave; or they have been hedged round with such punitively time-consuming terms and conditions that anyone not wedded solely to their job would find them impossible to maintain. In principle, the law is intended to give women an equivalent standing to men; in practice, it can make them an expensive option, and if organisations can find ostensibly non-discriminatory means of reducing their legal obligations, they may be tempted.

Everybody has read in the paper about a female miner or pilot or Chief Executive. We all know of women who earn more than men. But the media present a warped picture. Readers of the business pages get the profiles of highflyers, which pay homage to the stereotype either by glorying in it (teapots, kisses for husband, shapely legs), or by mentioning it and then kicking it firmly into touch. True, there are also statistics, but it's well-known that 'soft' data, such as anecdotes, impress people more than 'hard' data, such as figures. A human-interest story about the odd heroine who has arrived will be more compelling as evidence than an array of statistics showing how often women don't. The emphasis is on personal achievement, which cuts out non-heroines. It's easy to assume there are a lot of heroines, but they tend to be the same ones, time after time. I have lost count of the articles I have read about Anita Roddick, Margaret Thatcher, Yve Newbold, Virginia Bottomley. Exceptions become perceived as the norm, and the deadly file of depressing statistics remains comparatively low-profile.

In the news pages we get crises – and novelty items. Crises include cases of sexual harassment and sexual discrimination, sometimes sensational tales which invite character assassination of the women involved. Insinuations or 'evidence' about their sexual proclivities, or their racy leisure pursuits, or their incompetence, make each case a personal one rather than representative of themes which pervade the whole working world. The lack of context for novelty items can trivialise them: 'Wolf whistles banned by Islington Council: 400 men are being sent on a course to instil in them respect for their female colleagues by stopping them wolf-whistling and telling tales about sexual conquests.'

People who read women's magazines and women's pages and listen to *Woman's Hour* probably get a rounder view. Features here are aimed at the average woman rather than focusing on high achievers or protagonists in lawsuits. They are about being more assertive at work, how to increase your skills, how to return to work after having children, and how to have some time left for yourself when all duties are done. What men may see as faintly twee media campaigns about 'Being an expert juggler – managing home and work' are understood rather better by women as major triumphs of persistence over entropy. Stories of heroines and disasters are no proof that women have cracked the work issue. The facts, the statistics, the disparagement of women in some reports, and the dismissal of the concerns of average women, suggest strongly that we haven't.

'How can it be an issue? We have a woman on the Board.' This may be terrific, or it may be very dangerous. Does the existence of a woman on the Board necessarily validate every policy decision that emanates from it? Sometimes the woman is a token, a smokescreen to stop examination of the facts and the decision-making process. There may be plenty of goodwill, and an honest misconception based on too many assumptions. 'We do very well in our company. 85 per cent of our workforce are women.' Does quantity of females in the workplace imply quality of life? Who knows, unless somebody asks, and the answers are recorded and used? The quantity of women may only be a measure of the absence of alternatives for them elsewhere in the workplace. Or there may be a class element in play. 'Well, at blue-collar level we have little differentiation between the sexes. We've broken down the gender barriers quite well, and there are lots of ladies at the sharp end. At white-collar level, we don't have any ladies, it's true.'

Of course we should cheer as we pass each encouraging milestone on the way to a totally merit-based workplace; but we shouldn't confuse milestones with the end of the road. There's still a long, long way to go.

**COPOUT 4: The Hermaphrodite Solution.** Many men (and some women) deny making distinctions between the people they work with. 'It makes no difference to me what sex people are – I treat them all the same.' It's something they believe and are proud of, because it seems to demonstrate liberal attitudes to half the population, and the rejection of the old imbalance. But it leads them down the garden path: if people are all the same, any acknowledgment of difference has to be sexist (doesn't it?) – and therefore beneath contempt.

The motive for taking this tack is admirable, but the tack itself is misguided and premature. It is the result of interpreting 'equality' as 'sameness' – doublethink which results from far too narrow an interpretation of the aims of equal opportunities in the workplace. Believing that people should have equal opportunities and can offer equal value is a long way from believing that people are interchangeable. But in their zeal to be open and fair some people do, fuzzily, make this journey, arriving at a point which is a lot harder to defend, and can, paradoxically, make the task of women even more complex. Such an approach is bound to raise expectations that can't be fulfilled. If you can't acknowledge gender, not only do you lose a great chunk of personality, but you don't make allowances for differences of approach, thus increasing the chance of misunderstandings. You expect women to do things the normal way (i.e. the masculine way). If you're on the receiving end of this interpretation, you have no space to behave like a woman. One way out is to do your best to behave like a man, but because you are a woman you pay the price of embodying an unwelcome contradiction. Because the basic treatment meted out in the workplace is aimed at men, any appeal by women to be recognised as women becomes seen as tantamount to asking for special treatment, which is unprofessional and not fair, if they are claiming equal status. 'Are women equal members of the workforce or not? By making an issue out of this they undermine their own case.' Well, they are not equal members yet – either in numbers or in influence – and 'equal' ought to mean 'equally valid', not 'identical'. Discounting the fact that a person is a woman inhibits her performance and reduces the value of individuality. Acknowledging difference is *not* sexist, and the Hermaphrodite Solution, however well-meaning, is still a copout.

**COPOUT 5: You can't neutralise biology.** The Marketing Director of one international company wonders whether subtleties concerning gender at work are worth powder and shot. 'Surely, the crux of the great divide is that women have children and men don't – it's as simple as that. You can't neutralise biology.' His view is that biology sabotages 'working women' by means of two powerful weapons: children and hormones.

The problem with this man's stance is that it invests all women with features which belong to only some of them; characterises the features as negative; and conflates child-bearing with child-care, which need not be the exclusive preserve of women.

*The Patter of Tiny Feet*. There is no doubt that having children can obstruct women's career progress. 'They offered me a partnership,' says a solicitor of forty-something. 'Then I got pregnant, so they withdrew it and offered it to a man, even though I planned to carry on working.' It's not necessarily the existence of children which closes off paths, but unwarranted assumptions embraced by organisations:

- *Mothers are not reliable or committed.* They go home for tea and measles. (People who think like this are measuring commitment by quantity, not quality, and defining reliability as 'being instantly or constantly available', rather than 'making solid arrangements and keeping promises'.)
- *Mothers don't make lifelong employees.* (But the ten or fifteen years they may spend out of the workplace means there's a big chunk left of the 40-odd-year working life they can expect. And they may not take ten or fifteen years out.)
- *People who chop and change put organisations out of kilter.* (But they don't. People move on, even when they're male. Organisations profit by new ideas.)
- *Fathers need not be considered as caring parents.* (Ridiculous.)

The assumption that the slow progress of women at work is a knock-on effect from motherhood confines the search for solutions to technical matters involving maternity leave, the logistics of childcare, and the recruitment and training of women returners. All these matters are, indeed, important. 'Working mothers' bring benefits. Too often the stance is just the opposite: motherhood is a cost, not a value. But, as we've already mentioned, women fall behind in their careers long before they become mothers – and even if they don't have children. Slow progress for women at work is not just a gynaecological problem.

*The Hormone Trap.* Hormones, so it's thought, make women emotional, which tends to imply weepy, moody and unpredictable. One chap went further. His big problem with women, he said, was that they could make life dangerous. 'You get a woman on her period, right, and she's feeling grotty and 'orrible and steering a dirty great 250,000 ton ship along the English Channel – well, what are the chances of doing it safely? I wouldn't rate them high.'

Estimates of numbers vary, but some women don't experience menstrual tension, or pre-menstrual tension (PMT), at all. At the other end of the range are symptoms so extreme that they can be accepted by courts of law as extenuating circumstances in cases of murder, arson, or shoplifting. Somewhere in between is the average experience: a couple of days of depression, which will only be mildly grey and tetchy if things go well. True, if they don't, life is suddenly a problem. Staplers and other inanimate objects lie in wait to sabotage what you do. Everybody hates you – and no wonder, unattractive and bloated as you feel. Nothing goes right, and you think you can't cope. Somehow, you do, by fighting hard to behave rationally, however negative and self-critical you feel, knowing from experience that working on those days is more of an effort and the whole process feels worse. Luckily, some of the hormonal blues infest weekends, annual leave, and bank holidays, so not all the depression is on company time. The answer for most women is that they just get on with it, in much the same way as anyone battles through a week of sore throat, or stiff neck. It's just one of those things.

Stories about pre-menstrual tension being linked with klepto-mania and temporary incompetence may well be true, but they are certainly not universal. The problem with men's perception of the menstrual cycle is that it seems mysterious, unsafe and inconsistent – and these adjectives tend to stick to the people who experience it. The relevant question, however, is: does PMT reduce women's effectiveness? The answer is: probably not. Although many women do report being affected by PMT, there's little evidence that it influences the quality of their performance. It may affect how performance *feels* – but that's a different matter. A study of 217 female students found that most attributed some disruption of academic work to pre-menstrual symptoms. But menstruation had no effect on academic performance as measured by qualitative tests or exams.

Men are not immune from moody behaviour, and some research has even explored the possibility that levels of the male hormone, testosterone, are implicated – with, it has to be said, inconclusive results. Bad days can happen to anyone, with or without the effect of hormones. They can be caused by external disaster, virus, or simply getting out of bed on the wrong side. Days like these should be recognised, played down, and dropped into the gender-neutral category of days we can all experience.

Some women achieve public notice for extreme acts in which

hormone levels are quoted as a factor, and others suffer from lesser symptoms. To give all women the 'moodiness and unreliability' label is not warranted, any more than men's higher record of convictions for murder and violent crime, or their greater incidence of physically aggressive behaviour, proves that all men are sadistic and brutal.

The biology label is over-inclusive. It suggests that nothing which brainpower, upbringing, character or society can do will override something determined at birth. Using the biology label is a facile and fatalistic way of turning all gender issues into women's problems.

**COPOUT 6: Having their cake and eating it.** According to this argument, women are already getting far more than they deserve: women are exploiting the system, to the detriment of men, in demanding special treatment and work perks, despite their failure to match the standards of men. For instance, women get maternity leave, a privilege not open to men. They get equal pay, which isn't fair. One senior accountant said, bitterly, 'Female police officers of 5′ 2″ are less effective in a rough-house than men; they can't deal properly with a machete-wielding mob, and to pay them equal rates is a nonsense.' He seems to assume that the ability to deal effectively with a machete-wielding mob is the only criterion for being a good police officer, and that women are therefore inferior.

Such judgments are based entirely on masculine yardsticks, which tend to overlook male shortcomings; they blame women unreasonably for evidence of imbalance (*of course* there ought to be opportunities for paternity leave); they ignore the fact that legislation is often bypassed, so that women don't get what they are entitled to; and they neglect the value of the different contribution women can bring.

**COPOUT 7: Me too! or Well, we have to shave!** All the individual problems women raise are important, say some men, but they are not peculiar to women. It's just as hard being a man in a man's world. There's some truth in this, of course.

There are two chief ways of claiming kinship with women's experience. The first is not a copout. As men often point out, they themselves have to face considerable, but different, challenges *because* they are men, and therefore subject to all the expectations and demands which masculinity confers. Nobody would deny that the competitive and success-orientated expectation laid on men makes redundancy, for instance, not only a financial but a psychological threat; or that facing a situation in which your wife earns more than you do may be unbearable for men conditioned to be breadwinners. Such predicaments need to be handled with as much sympathy as the adversities which confront women.

The second argument is this: the challenges presented by work are not exclusive to women. Big brave macho men are prepared these days to confess that they feel nervous in meetings, too, and quail at the prospect of walking alone into bars to meet strangers. This, many men believe, helps them empathise with many of the difficulties that women face. Fair enough – but the copout starts if they also feel it entitles them to underplay the significance of what women report.

Specific circumstances may certainly create panic, or nerves, or depression, and of course there are areas of common experience. Life can be tough for anybody, and some people cope with it better than others, irrespective of gender. Confidence isn't exclusively men's preserve, or sensitivity women's. Both women and men may encounter crisis and feel stretched or fearful of a challenge. The overlap between men and women is sufficiently broad to make it foolish to categorise any individual on the basis of the stereotype

However, the sum of men's detrimental experience at work does not add up cumulatively to a total of oppression anything like that which women encounter. They are misguided if they expect women to deal with any situation just as staunchly as they would do. The working world is still their world, and they dominate in terms of numbers, power, influence and direction. The extra element for women is the chronic problem of trying to operate effectively in that world, which is not constructed to take account of the way they behave, and where, because of what they are, they may meet hostility, patronage, or incomprehension. For longevity and scope the difficulties are just not in the same league.

**COPOUT 8: Disarmament.** Many men are ruefully aware that too little is happening to facilitate women's progress in organisations. But sometimes frank admissions of inadequacy are a way of drawing women's fire on gender issues.

The method is to disarm those who challenge the status quo by agreeing with every word they say, and then do nothing to change matters. Confessions are made by men at all levels. 'No, we don't have any women on the Board. Perhaps we should.' Full stop. 'I know I'm a chauvinist [charming smile] and I expect you find what I say very sexist, my dear . . .' 'I have to admit that a lot of it is down to my ego – I think men are very selfish, much more selfish than women.' 'Yeah, life's tough for a woman. There's no doubt that whatever she does she has to be better than a man in the equivalent post.' 'We ought at least to put "women's issues" on the agenda once a year, like Health and Safety, before anybody waves a big stick at us, but it doesn't feel natural, somehow.'

It's so pleasant to hear – and it gets us nowhere by itself. True awareness of inequality, and genuine acceptance of the shared responsibility for putting it right, have to be combined with remedial action. Without action, the approach is no more than a superficial gambit to keep the conscience clear and temporarily shut up the opposition.

**COPOUT 9: Apocalypse now.** Gradually, over the years, men have undertaken a slow retreat from standpoint to standpoint in their view of women at work, and vestiges of every position they have ever taken up still remain. Once women were considered unsuitable for working life. Then they were acknowledged as competent, in general terms, but individual women came in for a lot of flak, the rationalisation being that their personalities were inadequate. That line of argument is dying, albeit slowly. The latest line of defence is to play on women's sense of cosmic guilt. Some men say they accept that women can do as good a job as men, more or less, but threaten catastrophic social ills as a consequence of their inclusion in the workplace or departure from the home. Here are three:

- House prices soar when women's salaries are taken into account for mortgages.
- Women priests will hit Church unity. ('Rent Asunder!' screamed the headlines when the General Synod voted narrowly in favour of admitting women to the priesthood in November 1992.)
- Juvenile crime is the fault of absentee mothers.

It won't wash, because it's back to front. What kind of economy works most effectively when half its contributors are excluded? What kind of unity characterises a Church which risks being damaged if half its parishioners are properly represented at operational level? What kind of juveniles are the result of virgin birth?

## Part Two: Cultivating a positive mindset

Men can choose to cultivate a more constructive attitude by combating three temptations: ridiculing and belittling experiences which they have never had, competing with women for the 'who's worst off' award, and relying on women to shield them from upset.

**Suspension of disbelief.** To combat all these negative influences, men need to see circumstances and comments from what, to them, is an alien point of view. Some men have sufficient self-knowledge to realise that they are blinkered by prejudice and stereotypes. 'I'm prepared to accept that my views on this are confused with a lot of personal baggage. It's going to take time for me to unpack that and see what it's about,' said one senior manager. Another remarked: 'I don't bring any insight. There are things I just don't understand. To me it's a bit like looking at Northern Ireland. The things that are happening there are rooted in stuff that's so deep-seated it's hard to untangle.' The other way of putting it, of course, is that actually the issues are brutally simple: it's *fixing them* that's hard. An obvious way of avoiding responsibility for fixing them is to claim that they are, in themselves, tremendously complex. Suspending disbelief must not be synonymous with suspending effort.

According to a female banker: 'Life is coloured with masculine characteristics and values.' To men they seem normal, the way things are meant to be, hallowed by practice. But what seems normal to men can look both masculine and optional to women. Women are not daft enough to accept or discard everything men live and work by. Their potential is in identifying where they can offer alternative perspectives and values. For that they need men to accept that an apparent universal 'given' can simply be the masculine option. Without a suspension of disbelief, an account of the challenges women face simply seems perverse: remote, irrelevant, unconnected to the reality men are familiar with. A young female barrister had a go at explaining the difficulty: 'It's so hard to articulate: where is the norm? It's nowhere near as drastic, but it's a bit like being a woman who's been beaten up for 25 years and then comes up in court in front of a male judge who wants to know exactly what the problem is. How is she supposed to tell how things ought to be in a world where you *don't* get beaten up? As a woman at work your sense of normality gets completely messed up. It's all cumulative – chipping away at things that aren't visible. You're oppressed by the subliminal effect of where you are and what you are. If you have a base of support you are freer to do things and function better. If I felt 100 per cent comfortable in chambers it would release another little bit of me.' Working out the appropriate balance in a mixed-sex workplace is a job for both sexes. If it's asking too much of a man for him to believe straight off that organisational culture restricts women, he can at least suspend his disbelief long enough to weigh up the evidence. Men should start by assuming that women are not self-indulgently whingeing; not uttering a blanket condemnation of all men by means of exaggerated reports of man's inhumanity to woman; but making an honest attempt to identify closed thinking and contribute something new.

**Quantum of tolerance.** Men also need a quantum of tolerance. A male Personnel Director explained: 'I think men have a level of forgiveness for other men that they don't apply to women; in the same way women are more tolerant with other women. What we need to do is extend it between the sexes, but for that we need a deeper understanding of why men and women behave as they do.'

He was not advocating sympathy for weakness, but a flexible approach to another stand-point which will encourage openness rather than shutting it off.

With a quantum of tolerance men will listen beyond the point at which they think they have the definitive answer. You may be a Prince, Sir, but, believe me, working life is full of men who aren't. I told Charles, a highly accessible senior manager, about James, who had committed a peculiarly extreme example of old-fashioned discrimination. Charles's first – stunningly discouraging – reaction was that I was making it all up for effect. It took time to convince him that a brother man could have behaved in the way I described. Eventually, he commented: 'Well, James has got a problem, hasn't he?' He certainly has – but women can't be quite so dismissive of him as Charles can: he's not attacking men. James's problem is also women's problem – and, indeed, Charles's problem.

With a quantum of tolerance from both men and women difficulties will become more manageable. Strategies for getting along in a different way may seem unnatural and artificial to start with, like struggling to learn a new language. But they will become more spontaneous with practice and habit.

**Where I go, ego.** In the book *Families and how to survive them* Robin Skynner tells John Cleese about the difficulties which trained female therapists encounter, in confronting men about the façade they have put up to hide their perceived inadequacies. 'There's another interesting point about this male vulnerability,' he says. 'It's astonishing how considerate and protective women are towards it . . . they'd often let the husband get away with murder, and then tell me afterwards how angry he made them feel . . . At first they find it terribly difficult to put a man to the test. It's as if they've been trained from birth to avoid it . . . It's astonishing – this womanly need to protect the male ego seems to be one of the most deeply ingrained inhibitions of all.'

I don't want to be nasty. I don't want to visit the sins of the fathers on the sons. I'm ready to stand up to bigots, buffoons and bastards, however frightening they may be. But there are all the other chaps who are none of these things, and who are inoculated, by their own decency and that of the women they deal with, against any realisation that a disease exists. Some suffer badly from 'Me too' syndrome, like this retail store manager: 'Women are terribly unfair. They count on men's gentlemanly instincts. They don't take on board men's vulnerabilities and problems.' Codswallop. We do, we do. That's why we grin and bear it, even though it hurts. Many women (including me) are inhibited by a mighty urge to shelter men from their own fragility. We seem to feel we're tough enough to take assaults on our own identity, yet we doubt men's capacity to do the same, so we help them keep up the act in order to fend off their feelings of inadequacy. We know *we* can survive, but we don't know if *they* can, so we choose not to put them to the test.

Things which need to change will be easier to identify if men invite comment from women about the things that they do, and at the same time make it unnecessary for women to protect them from threats to their masculinity. Men need to tell themselves what they so often tell women: 'Don't take it so personally!' If they are hurt, defensive, shocked, or unmanned because of what women say, some women will stop saying it, and men will learn nothing; others will say it louder, and that will hurt worse.

## Part Three: Rules of Thumb

**Provide support on women's terms.** Men need to be more supportive of women. They often are already, but sometimes it's support on their terms, not women's. The key to support is maintaining dialogue. Men *tell* women to believe in themselves, but they don't always supply support in a form in which women can use it. It may be a question of comparing terms and understandings, compiling a phrasebook to minimise misreadings.

A senior woman: 'I gave a presentation to a group of four women and two men. The women listened, nodded at appropriate points. It helped the flow. It didn't necessarily mean they agreed with me, but that they respected my point of view and reserved comment until invited to speak. My confidence was enhanced by them – and demolished by the men, who challenged every point I made just when they felt like it, so that I lost track of my argument and felt I'd suddenly become involved in a fight rather than a co-operative venture. I got less and less fluent and convincing. Afterwards I tried to explain this to the men. They were shocked. They had been, they said, involved and absorbed in the unfolding of the scenario, and were showing support by making it abundantly clear that they were on board. They saw strength, so they challenged it, in the expectation of increased strength in response. They didn't get it – but we'll all know better next time.' The environment may seem antagonistic to women even when it isn't meant to be. Men have to show they're on board without challenging too harshly. Women have to understand that challenge can be constructive and that it doesn't necessarily mean hostility.

**Create an accepting environment.** Half the responsibility for maintaining dialogue between the sexes – and making it effective – is men's. 'I've no objection to having a woman on the team, but she'll have to be pretty strong-minded,' said a systems manager. 'If things go wrong, that's her problem, same as it would be if it was a man, with a different style of working from the rest. Any woman has to be able to face the challenge of the team, even if they're all dyed-in-the-wool MCPs.' Not sensible. In a team, it's never the sole responsibility of any member to make it work, and it's ludicrous to expect one member of it to 'win' a respect that there is no pressure on team-mates to offer. Nor is it only the leader's responsibility to make it work; the members have to pull their weight. If it doesn't work, they've got no business to blame the leader and absolve themselves.

'Women won't fit' and 'women are totally responsible for their own integration' are both shortsighted and irresponsible forms of discrimination. Men must pay active attention to ways in which they can help the process of assimilation.

**Take a lower profile.** One male manager I know regularly attends meetings at which the other four or five contributors are women. In contrast to other meetings he attends at which more men are present, at these the natural dynamic is for him to take over. So he has adopted a deliberate policy of maintaining a low profile: instead of putting in his two-penn'orth, doing most of the talking and re-setting the agenda as he goes, he sits quiet so that others can have their say. It's 'abnormal' behaviour for him, and his concern is whether his personal contribution is sufficiently high. The women, who have grown to expect him regularly to punctuate proceedings with a view or a challenge, are simultaneously discomfited by being thrown back on their own devices to generate ideas, and delighted that they can pursue a more congenial pattern. His reason for persisting, despite discomfort all round, is that an audience of five for a single speaker generates fewer creative solutions than the sum of six contributions. If one contribution had been enough, there would have been no grounds for calling the meeting.

**Learn alternative methods of communication.** Men and women know the nuances of their own universes, and women probably understand men's universe better than men understand women's, because women adapt more to men when men are around. If there's one message in this book, it's that both men and women have a responsibility to help women get to the point where they can be judged on merit. Here are some simple communication clues for men:

- Ask women questions to give them a chance to elaborate on what they say.
- Ask them how they feel about things. Tell them how you feel.
- Don't assume you have to provide an answer or a solution for every comment they make.
- When they are talking – look at them! Many men listen intently, but turn away to do so, where another woman would watch the speaker's face to pick up every scrap of the message. It feels like a diminution of attention when there's no eye contact.
- Stop talking and signal that it's the woman's turn – often! Women are less likely than men to interrupt you when you're in full flow, even if they have a contribution which could be valuable.

- Be gentle in manner, if rigorous in challenge. Of course women's ideas need testing. But they don't need testing to destruction, taking the women along with them. It may be enough simply to state what you are doing: 'I find your argument very compelling, but I'd like to push it a bit further . . .'
- Reassure women that they are adding value – if they are. Part of the reward for women is in the dialogue itself, and it's a rich source of motivation if they feel they are contributing well.
- Tell women if their response confuses you.
- If you decide to play things differently, ask them to tell you whether it works. 'Was that a sexist comment? Have I taken over? Did I interrupt?'
- Don't be fazed by the absence of the bullshit factor. Look for the nuggets, not the packing.

**Try it with men.** By maintaining dialogue with women men may also learn the advantages of listening and questioning, and therefore increase their understanding not only of women, but of other men. This should lead to fewer feelings of isolation all round. It may often be women who spotlight the softer values, but they're not confined to women. Many men respond enthusiastically to a stronger emphasis on the social currents and feelings which under-pin decision and action.

**Ask yourself: is there more to life than this?** Busy busy busy. British men are more workaholic than most. Forty-two per cent put in 46 hours a week, compared with 14 per cent of Germans, according to a report by the Equal Opportunities Commission. Many men suffer stress from the demands of their job, exacerbated by the only way they know of facing up to it: they inhibit emotion, rely on aggression, power and control, and become obsessed with success. The *Financial Times* of 17 August 1992 quoted a survey which showed that 97 per cent of executives felt that on their way to the top they had had to make sacrifices. Many felt that their work was damaging their personalities, their work relationships, their friendships, and their home life. One in five assessed the effect as serious. These managers estimated that 70 per cent of executives in their organisations are also victims of stress, displaying symptoms such as bad temper, irritability, nervous breakdowns, heart attacks, and rattling the change in their pockets.

Identifying solely with work probably shortens life. Men who throw all their energies into work paint themselves into a corner where they have no opportunity to be or learn anything else. This feels like security for as long as the economy remains stable, and technology doesn't change any more work practices, and life-partners don't have other ideas. But if the unpredictable happens, too forceful a concentration on work wildly increases men's vulnerability.

It's dangerous to ignore the status of non-work demands within life as a whole. In the near future, there will be more elderly people in the community, and fewer young ones of working age. Somebody has to keep the home fires burning, but it needn't be women. The crossover between work and home will need to be substantially re-evaluated by both men and women if their needs, plus those of their dependants and the organisations they work for, are all to be considered.

Men have the opportunity to ask themselves big questions. Are you sure working for pay is all that makes you what you are? That you can't gain satisfaction and a sense of contribution in a wider sphere? That you'll *never* be called upon to revise your priorities? Men who answer 'Yes . . . Yes . . . Yes . . .' are blindly denying that they're free – and may be forced – to develop in new directions. Such possibilities for personal growth open up territory for exploration far beyond the question of women's status at work.

# Afterword

I don't expect a hassle-free working life. But I don't want to be a stranger in a strange land until I retire. If I have to face stress and discomfort I'd like it to come from the job itself, not from the struggle to address the task effectively in the first place. And I'd like to see stronger, clearer, more productive connections all round, between men and women, families and individuals, work and life.

We can carry on living in Never-Never-Land – or we can solve the problems which plague us. There isn't just one problem, and there won't be just one solution. Everyone – male or female, at work or not – can contribute to managing a more effective interplay between men, women and organisations. If we do, the jackpot is a 'win/win/win' result. If we fail to untangle the complicated skein of social, sexual and psychological threads which tie us all in knots, what we end up with is 'lose/lose/lose'. From an idealistic standpoint there are no other combinations: if *anybody* loses, *nobody* wins.

Of the possible alternative futures, the worst-case scenario is one which not only maintains all the most negative aspects of the current state of play, but allows them to spiral into more destructive complications. Men, perhaps believing that they have no option but to choose a ladder and climb it, perhaps dazzled by the meretricious allure of old, narrow definitions of success, pay several prices. They can climb stressed and blinkered up the ladder until they fall off into oblivion, dropping dead as they hit retirement. They can close off options for extending themselves, so that if forces outside their control jolt the ladder, they find no alternative resource. Their offer to their families is limited to brief moments spared from the climb, which perpetuates for their children the restrictive stereotypes that forced them on to the ladder in the first place.

For women, the worst of all possible worlds is a selection of ghettoes where they can be outsiders, clones or drones – plus an increase in the difficulty of crossing the widening gulfs between them. The number of women in the workplace will grow, but women will continue to be outsiders judged against inappropriate norms and found wanting, facing continued male prejudice, subject to minor hassles and major injustices. Or they will have to defend themselves by becoming clones of men, to the point where they dutifully appropriate men's style and men's tunnel vision, and follow them into the pit of stress and overwork. At the same time, if women continue to be exclusively held responsible for child-rearing, flexible working and provisions for child-care become pricey privileges which organisations can avoid by employing men. This confirms men in their restricted option of Breadwinner's ladder, and creates the third ghetto for women. Women can carry on providing their immeasurable contribution to the community by being mothers and housewives; however, value remains vested in 'work' – all the more as 'working women' become more visible and more influential. So women who choose to play their part by bringing up a family find they still receive negligible recognition or reward, and, being neither men nor 'working women', are perceived twice over as drones.

In the worst case, the consumer society continues to measure quality of life in terms of what you can buy. True, people in households which need two incomes to subsist have very limited options. Others may have more control over the level at which they choose to survive – but fail to exercise it. Instead of adding enjoyment to life, work simply becomes a means of earning purchasable consolation prizes for the precious intangibles it subtracts – peace, friendship, fun, moments for reflection.

People under pressure don't offer all their creative potential to the organisations which employ them. At times of rapid change, elasticity of thinking and flexible people are vital assets. Organisations without elastic get caught with their pants round their ankles.

On the other hand, if men and women embrace change and are willing to take positive action, there are more hopeful possibilities. Under the win/win/win scenario, parallel universes begin to dovetail. Women reach a critical mass at levels where they start to provide equally valid role-models for younger men and women. It's valuable to be different, and to live in peaceful co-existence. We know enough about the way the other half works to understand when things don't go quite the way we expect. Experience and open discussion teach men how to interpret women, and women men. Anyone can take part, and it's exciting when the unpredictable produces constructive change.

The Big World and the Small World become Real Worlds for both women and men. Neither women nor men are victims at work; men aren't visitors at home. The workplace and the home are equally fulfilling for men and women; there's universal recognition of valuable, visible contributions to both. There's freedom to step outside the frame of expectation. We can choose to change direction, in partnership with other people at home and at work. None of us is at the mercy of stereotypes – and we aren't recreating them, even unto the third and fourth generations.

Times change, people change, their needs change, their offer changes. Work affects life, and life affects work. Whether simultaneously or consecutively, the choice exists not only to be measured by what you *do*, but also to spend time on *being*. Do – be – do – be – do. Instead of continuously suffering as scapegoats of the system, under constant pressure to prove worth and justify existence by flagging up notable achievement after notable achievement, we can stop and stare without penalty, work out what it's all for – and then leap back, refreshed, into the fray (if we want to), carolling: dooby dooby doo!

The most stubborn resistance to a win/win/win outcome is likely to come from men. Short-term, they may see it as being in their interest not to alter the status quo – or they may simply not realise what they're missing. However, it's inevitable that women will acquire more influence in the workplace. Women are already changing things at work and at home, because they have to or because they want to, and men will simply not be able to maintain the roles or the self-images to which they cling. They will be forced to re-assess where they stand. But because we're symbiotic, unless there's a true choice for women, there can't be one for men.

I want to be one of many women who can choose to change things: to shape rather than adapt, create rather than adjust, act rather than react, in the belief that the gain for us all will be startling. There are two ways of creating the options: like ripping a plaster off hairy skin, either slow and painful, or fast and painful. Absence of pain might suggest not enough was changing. It's worth enduring some pain. It's even worth watching men endure some.

But has it got to be a battlefield? That's not what I want – nor is it the most effective way to get results. It's not as though every woman's presence at work implied victory over a rejected man. The only defeat is for people of either sex who are not competent to perform the tasks organisations demand. I've never understood the sense behind fighting wars to achieve peace. I'd rather use less confrontational methods. However, so often they don't work: sweet moderation is interpreted as weakness, and hammered; temperate behaviour is ignored as inconsequential; constructive criticism is met with defensiveness or disparagement.

Do I have to counter accusations that I'm whingeing by being abrasive, outrageous, difficult? Do I have to adopt the most extremist of men's tactics – aggression, defensiveness, hostility, pre-emptive strikes, even violence? It seems hypocritical and paradoxical to do so, and then turn round and say: 'Right, I've won, and now I can be a proper woman again.' But will I get anywhere if I don't? Do I have to be a terrorist, uncouth and brutal, to be heard?

Or can we sit down and talk about it, woman to man, man to woman?

# Key Sources and Further Reading

**Chapter 2: How the Other Half Work**

Archer, John and Lloyd, Barbara, *Sex and Gender*, Penguin Books Ltd, 1982.

Hammond, Valerie, *Gender: What does the research tell us?*, Target – Management Development Review **Vol 5 no 1**, 6–7, 1992.

Hargreaves, David J and Colley, Ann J (eds), *The Psychology of Sex Roles*, Harper and Row, London, 1986.

Heatherington, I, Crown, J, Wagner, H and Rigby, S, *Toward an understanding of social consequences of feminine immodesty about personal achievements*, Sex Roles **20**, 371–380, 1989.

Nicholson, John, *Men and Women: How Different are they?*, OUP, 1993.

Vanucci, Tricia and Kleiner, Brian H, *Understanding and coping with the fear of success*, Women in Management Review and Abstracts, **Vol 5 no 2**, 1990.

**Chapter 3: Interpreting the Other Half**

Dion, KL and Schuller, RA, *Ms and the Manager: A tale of two stereotypes*, Sex Roles **22**, 469–577, 1990.

Egolf, DB and Corder, LE, *Height differences of low and high job status, female and male corporate employees*, Sex Roles **24**, 365–373, 1991.

Simkins-Bullock, JA and Wildman, BG, *An investigation into the relationships between gender and language*, Sex Roles **24**, 149–160, 1991.

Tannen, Deborah, *You Just Don't Understand*, Virago Press Limited, 1992.

**Chapter 4: Measuring Up**

Alban Metcalf, Beverly, 'Different Gender – Different Rules?', *Managing Organisations in 1992: Strategic Response*, Peter Barrer and Cary L Cooper (eds), Routledge, 1991.

Alfred Marks Bureau Ltd, *The Boss: A Quantitative Report on secretaries' attitudes and experiences*, PO Box 311, Borehamwood, Herts, WD6 1WD, 1991.

Archer, John, *Sex bias in evaluations at college and work*, The Psychologist 5, 200–204, 1992.

Eagly, AH and Johnson, BT, *Gender and Leadership Style: a meta-analysis*, Psychological Bulletin **108**, 233–256, 1990.

Eagly, AH and Karau, SJ, *Gender and the emergence of Leaders: a meta-analysis*, Journal of Personality and Social Psychology **60**, 685–710, 1991.

Eskilson, A and Wiley, M Glenn, *Sex Composition and Leadership in small groups*, Sociometry **39**, 183–194, 1976.

Gilligan, C, *In a Different Voice*, Harvard University Press, Cambridge Massachusetts, 1982.

Horgan, Dianne D, *A Cognitive Learning Perspective on Women becoming expert managers*, Women in Management Review and Abstracts **Vol 5 No 2**, 1990.

Jackson, Charles and Hirsh, Wendy, *Women Managers and Career Progression: The British Experience*, Women in Management Review and Abstracts **Vol 6 No 2**, 1991.

Kohlberg, L, *Stage and Sequence: The cognitive-developmental approach to socialization*, In DA Goslin (ed) Handbook of Socialization Theory and Research. Chicago: Rand McNally, 1969.

**Chapter 5: Big World, Small World, Real World**

*1990 General Household Survey*; *1991 General Household Survey*, Office of Population Censuses and Surveys HMSO.

Archer, John, *Childhood Gender Roles: Structure and Development*, The Psychologist **Vol 2 No 9**, 1989.

Cassidy, ML and Warren, BO, *Status consistency and work satisfaction among professional and management women and men*, Gender and Society 5, 193–206, 1991.

Corse, Sara J, *The Influence of a Manager's Pregnancy on Hierarchical Relationships*, Women In Management Review and Abstracts **Vol 6 No 4**, 1991.

Eisler, RM and Blalock, JA, *Masculine Gender Role Stress: Implications for the assessment of men*, Clinical Psychology Review 1991 **11** (1), 45–60.

Holton, Victoria, *The Female Resource – an overview*, Ashridge Management Research Group, 1989.

Lewis, Suzan, *Dual-Career Families in the UK: An Update*, Women In Management Review and Abstracts **Vol 6 No 4**, 1991.

Rapoport, R and Rapoport, RN, *The Dual-Career Family: A Variant Pattern and Social Change* Human Relations **Vol 22**, 3–30, 1969.

Rosin, Hazel M and Korabik, Karen, *Workplace Variables, affective responses, and intention to leave among women managers*, Journal of Occupational Psychology **64**, 317–330, 1991.

### Chapter 6: Close Encounters
Adsearch *Sexual Harassment in the Office: A Quantitative Report on Client attitudes and experiences*, Alfred Marks Bureau, 1991.
Adsearch *Sexual Harassment in the Office: A Quantitative Report on Employee attitudes and experiences*, Alfred Marks Bureau, 1991.
Anderson, CJ and Fisher, C, *Male-female relationships in the workplace: perceived motivation in office romance*, Sex Roles **25**, 163–180, 1991.
Institute of Personnel Management, *Statement on Harassment at Work*, IPM House, Camp Road, Wimbledon London SW19 4UX, 1992.
Saal, FE, Johnson, CB, and Weber, N, *Friendly or sexy? It may depend on whom you ask*, Psychology of Women Quarterly **13** (3), 263–276, 1989.

### Chapter 7: Narrowing the Acceptability Gap
Hammond, Valerie and Holton, Viki, *A Balanced Workforce? Achieving cultural change for women: a comparative study*, Ashridge Management Research Group, 1991.
MacDonald, Isobel, *Women's Development at BBC Scotland*, Executive Development **Vol 5 No 1**, 1992.
*Cases for Women's Development*, Target – Management Development Review **Vol 5 No 2**, 32–34, 1992

### Chapter 8: Women: A Gender For Change
O'Leary, Virginia E and Johnson, Judy L, *Steep Ladder, Lonely Climb. Breaking through the Glass Ceiling*, Women in Management Review and Abstracts **Vol 6 No 5**, 1991.

### Chapter 9: Men: A Gender For Change
Skynner Robin and Cleese John, *Families and How to survive them*, Mandarin, London, 1983

# Index